THE SWEDISH WAY
TO TENNIS SUCCESS

THE SWEDISH WAY TO TENNIS SUCCESS

Mark Cox and Dennis Gould

Arthur Barker
An imprint of Weidenfeld (Publishers) Limited, London

First published in Great Britain in 1990 by
Weidenfeld and Nicolson Limited
91 Clapham High Street, London SW4 7TA

Text copyright © Mark Cox and Dennis Gould
Illustrations copyright © Peter Bull

British Library Cataloguing in Publication Data
Cox, Mark
    The Swedish way to tennis success.
    1. Lawn tennis. Techniques
    I. Title   II. Gould, Dennis
    796.3422
ISBN 0–213–85005–2

Printed in Great Britain by
Butler & Tanner Ltd, Frome and London

**(Frontispiece) Stefan Edberg after his Wimbledon
Men's Singles win in 1988.**

Contents

Illustrations

Acknowledgements

The compilation of this book would not have been possible without the help of many people. A number of officials at the Swedish Tennis Association, in Stockholm, have smoothed the way for me; in particular, Krister Hjerpe. Also in Stockholm, Percy and Harry Rosberg at SALK made valuable contributions, as did Sten Heyman. Tor Lovén at the Swedish Tennis Instructors Association provided me with a considerable amount of material. In Uppsala, I am indebted to Hasse Olsson for sharing with me his experiences and opinions as a Swedish Davis Cup Team Captain and to Hans Nytell for supplying much information about Minitennis in Sweden. In Båstad, the hospitality of Dagny Nilsson made it easier to obtain a lot of historical information from Prof. Eve Malmquist and to meet with Björn Hellberg, who is so knowledgeable about Swedish tennis statistics. Also in Båstad, Bengt Cronvall and coaching staff at Tretorn Tennis Academy, made me most welcome. Lars Ryberg provided me with a helpful insight into psychological aspects of training.

Those involved with tennis often lead busy lives, travelling around the world, and so I am very grateful to those who were helpful in sparing time to assist with my research. Amongst the Swedes were Ove Bengtsson, Lennart Bergelin, Leif Dahlgren, Sven Davidson, Birger Folke, Bengt Grive, Carl-Axel Hageskog, Anders Järryd, Jan-Erik Lundqvist, John-Anders Sjögren and Jonas Svensson. In England, I received assistance from Jeremy Bates, Dan Maskell, Alan Little at the Wimbledon Lawn Tennis Museum, and Danny Marsh.

My daughters, Elisabet, Karen and Kristina, kept we well supplied with up-to-date information from Sweden, as did my brother-in-law, Bengt Hellman. My wife, Inga-Lisa is always supportive and sometimes acts as a 'living dictionary'.

To all these people I express my gratitude ... and to my co-author, Mark Cox, who has encouraged and guided me with his expertise.

Dennis E. Gould.

Foreword

It was at the Båstad Tennis Stadium that I first met Dennis Gould. Sweden had just beaten Yugoslavia to enter the Davis Cup Final for the seventh time. I was interested to hear that he and Mark Cox were writing a book about the successes of Swedish tennis.

I could tell from his command of Swedish and his knowledge of the country and the sport that Dennis was well qualified to carry out his research. Mark Cox is, of course, a well-known name in Swedish tennis circles, especially since he won the Stockholm Open Singles title in 1976. More recently, I had met him in his role as BBC TV commentator. I was, therefore, very pleased to be asked to contribute this Foreword.

The authors have combined their skills and interest in tennis to produce a book which examines the many factors which may have attributed to the quite amazing growth in the reputation of Swedish tennis. From lessons which may be learnt at national level to tips for clubs and coaches, we are led to a skillful examination, by Mark, of the techniques by which some of my fellow-countrymen have become well-known. Anyone who is seriously seeking to improve his or her game, surely cannot fail to do so if they follow this advice.

But, in the long run, there is really nothing miraculous about the so-called 'Swedish Tennis Miracle'. It is the result of a combination of many things, as the authors of this book explain: tradition and inspiration, determination, will-to-win and concentration, physical and mental conditions, facilities, organization, coaching and much more. I would like to add the ability to put up with the travel and other non-glamorous, non-playing aspects of the game, plus plenty of good luck!

From my early days at a small club in Lidköping and winning the Swedish Junior Outdoor Championship as a sixteen-year-old in 1977, it had been my ambition, as it has been for thousands of other players, to win at Wimbledon. When that dream came true in 1989 and John Fitzgerald and I won the Men's Doubles title, it meant that I had won in all four Grand Slam events. All the hard work had been well worthwhile!

You may not aspire to such complete dedication to the game, but this book should help you to experience the success of improvement. Good luck!

Anders Järryd

Anders Järryd in full flight

Introduction

When a book has a co-authorship, it may present some difficulties. The reader may wonder about the contribution made by each of the partners, whilst the authors are faced with the problem of who shall present the material and how. Let us try to clarify that straight away.

This co-operation has not been in the nature of ghost-writing. Both of us are intrigued by the phenomenon of Swedish success in tennis in the last decade or so. Both of us, separately and privately, have given some thought to seeking an explanation, or a combination of reasons which go part way towards explaining such success. We converge on the puzzle from different directions.

Mark Cox is well-known in the circles of British Lawn Tennis and far beyond these shores. Younger enthusiasts who are less aware of his past attainments on court will be more likely, perhaps, to recognize his name as a BBC TV commentator on this sport. Amongst his many other achievements, it is appropriate to mention here that he won the Stockholm Open Tournament in 1976, beating Jimmy Connors on the way and Manuel Orantes in the final. He thus shares the honour of winning this Grand Prix title with such players as Nicola Pilic, Stan Smith, Arthur Ashe, John McEnroe and Boris Becker, and with the Swedish stars Björn Borg, Mats Wilander and Stefan Edberg.

Mark is now actively engaged with the Lawn Tennis Association in his role of National Training Coach.

Mark also holds the distinction of being the first amateur to beat a professional after the game became 'open' in 1968. At the tournament in Bournemouth, Mark defeated Pancho Gonzales. Incidentally, it was the Swedish Tennis Association which was a prime mover in bringing about open tennis.

I bring to the partnership forty years' knowledge of Sweden and things Swedish, an even longer love of the game of lawn tennis and perhaps most importantly the time, made available by the luxury of retirement, to devote to the research and writing.

The 'pinnacle' of my achievements in tennis was the captaincy of my teacher training college VI. Whilst at college I obtained an LTA Proficiency Certificate and subsequently did some coaching. My professional training and marriage to a Swedish wife eventually led me to become principal of a multinational school in Stockholm.

Mark and I first met at the Stockholm Open in 1971. Mark was playing and I was a spectator. In the second round, Mark was due to play against the winner of a match going on between Franulovic and a young player named Björn Borg. This young player was already beginning to earn a name for himself and here he was performing in front of his home supporters. After Borg had won the first set, Mark had mingled with the spectators and wandered round behind the court to have a look at the performance of the lad he might be meeting in the next round.

Mark Cox, winner of the Stockholm Open Tournament in 1976.

Recognizing Mark, and reacting in a way that many people do when they meet a fellow-countryman outnumbered and surrounded by 'foreigners', I approached him and wished him good luck in the next round. We discussed Borg's performance and chatted about life in Stockholm and Sweden in general. But Franulovic won the next two sets and so beat this Swede who was to become one of the world's best-ever tennis players. In fact, Björn was not beaten by a player younger than himself until seven years later, by John McEnroe in the semi-final of this same Stockholm Open tournament.

Several years later, I heard Mark's observations from the BBC TV commentators' box, as Mats Wilander added success to success, as several other Swedes did well, as Sweden won in Davis Cup matches and then Stefan Edberg won the coveted crown of the Wimbledon men's singles championship in 1988. I now had time to tell the story of Sweden's success and to examine possible explanations. I wondered if Mark would like to join me in the project.

It transpired that Mark, like many others, had wondered about this very question. He has the added advantage of having played many times in Sweden and has met most of the Swedish players. He knows many of their star performers both on and off the court. He had his own theories about possible explanations of this phenomenon and was keen to know if there were lessons from which others could learn, but the life of a professional tennis coach is a busy, hectic one. It involves much travelling and is not very conducive to tackling authorship.

Thus the contributions have fused, complementing each other, to produce the book in this format. I have brought my knowledge and contacts with Sweden and Swedish tennis to supplement Mark's expert knowledge of the game and its players. I have compiled the text, but it has been with the help and guidance of Mark from start to finish.

I hope that we have provided food for thought and inspiration to those who are at all interested in the sport of tennis and who admire and wonder over Sweden's achievements.

Dennis Gould

PART I

The Swedish Miracle
by Dennis Gould

Sweden's success in tennis

The achievements of Swedish men players in recent years has been called the 'miracle' of Swedish tennis. The name which first springs to mind is that of Björn Borg. He won the men's singles title at Wimbledon a record number of times. The previous record for successive victories in the modern tournament had been held by Fred Perry. The Englishman had won in 1934, 1935 and 1936. Borg equalized this number of Wimbledon singles titles and went on to reach the phenomenal total of five in 1980.

Even so, that achievement, great as it was, does not in itself constitute the 'miracle'. What seemed even more incredible was the fact that so closely after Björn Borg had finally failed to continue his invincible command of top tennis titles and had lost to John McEnroe in the Wimbledon final that would have given the Swede his sixth successive win, another young compatriot won a Grand Slam title, the French Open. The victor there, Mats Wilander, was still only seventeen years old. He went on rapidly to win several more Grand Slam titles, so that within only a few more years, apart from the much publicized and highly regarded Wimbledon record, his achievements stood comparison with those of the great Björn himself.

Before the age of majority, Mats had won four

Björn Borg, the best-known Swedish tennis player past and present, and the inspiration for the players who have come after him.

Grand Slam titles, a unique achievement. Also unequalled were his victories in both the Swedish Open and the Stockholm Open in the same year. That was in 1983 when he also reached the top position in Grand Prix world rankings.

Yet more remarkable was the fact that Wilander was not the only Swede at the top of the game. Mats has not yet emulated Borg in winning Wimbledon; instead, that honour has gone to another Swede, Stefan Edberg, in 1988.

These two young players vied with each other for the top positions on the world-ranking lists. Stefan Edberg held the number two position at the start of the 1988 season, one place above Mats Wilander. At the end of that year, the final ranking showed Mats Wilander as the leader, as number one. Towards the end of 1989, Edberg was ranked as number three whereas Wilander had slipped down a dozen or so places.

In the years before Sweden started to gain successes internationally, there had never been more than one or two top players in the country. Björn Borg in his heyday was far beyond the reach of other Swedish competitors. Now, however, there was 'depth' developing in Swedish tennis talent. In 1973 there had been four Swedish players good enough to be included in the officially recognized world-ranking list. By 1987 that figure had risen to fifty-seven.

Not only were Edberg and Wilander taking it in turns at the top of ranking lists, but when

Mats was number one at the end of 1988 half of those named in the first half-dozen were Swedes. Lesser-known Kent Carlsson had risen to sixth position. In fact, there were twelve Swedes in the top one hundred, that much sought-after position of prestige.

It is interesting to note that Stefan Edberg and Mats Wilander both come from the province of Sweden called Småland. This is a very rugged part of the country and the hard-working people who live in that region, the Smålänningar, have gained a reputation for their determined doggedness. They have had to struggle and never had things easy. So it is not surprising that there is considerable regional pride. They were not slow to point out, in May 1988, when Britain was pleased to see that both Jeremy Bates and Andrew Castle were in the top one hundred of the ATP ranking list (in the sixties and nineties respectively), that their little province alone had four players in that position. In addition to their star representatives, Edberg and Wilander, Jan Gunnarsson was in the fifties and Niclas Kroon in the eighties. Subsequently, Kroon won his first Grand Prix singles title at Brisbane in October 1989 and followed that by reaching the semi-final in the Sydney Indoor Championship. Consequently, at the time that he became the first Swede to strike a ball in the Stockholm Open Tournament, in November 1989 at its new Globe venue, he had reached his best-ever ranking position at fifty. Gunnarsson's ranking had also risen after reaching the semi-final of the Australian Open and by the start of the Stockholm Open he had climbed to number thirty-six; his surprise defeat of Boris Becker raised him even further.

The depth of Swedish talent was demonstrated at the French Open in 1986, when the known Swedish stars were knocked out of the tour-nament one after the other: Nyström, Edberg, Järryd and Wilander. But Swedish interest was kept very much alive by the fine performance of the less renowned Mikael Pernfors who went right through to the final, where he was ultimately defeated by Ivan Lendl.

In that fabulous season of 1986, Swedish players competed in the finals of no less than 44 per cent of the Grand Prix titles played for, all around the world. After the 1989 season, statistics show that Sweden now has sixteen players who have won GP singles titles. There are about seventy of these prestigious men's professional tournaments played annually all around the world. Altogether Swedish players have gained 160 such victories, with Björn Borg having by far the largest share (sixty-two) which is thirty more than Mats Wilander has, so far! Stefan Edberg and Joakim Nyström are the others with more than ten. Six players have, to date, won only once, but they contribute to this confirmation of depth of high-level talent.

Records show that on the middle day of July 1989 there were no fewer than six Swedish finalists playing in top-ranking tournaments around the world.

The depth of Swedish talent was demonstrated once again at the Stockholm Open, in November 1989. Amongst the forty-eight entrants in the singles were non-Swedish stars like Ivan Lendl, Boris Becker, Andre Agassi, Aaron Krickstein, Alberto Mancini, Tim Mayotte and Yannick Noah; yet seven Swedes remained amongst the last sixteen and Ivan

(Right) Mats Wilander, United States Open champion, 1988.

(Overleaf) The Davis Cup final, Sweden v West Germany, 1989.

Lendl was the only non-Swede in the semi-finals.

The impressive Swedish record revealed by tennis statistics does not confine itself to men's singles. The highest rated men's doubles player, at the conclusion of the 1988 rankings, was the Swedish Davis Cup star, Anders Järryd. At the beginning of November 1989 he was in first position in the Nabisco Grand Prix standings and in their doubles teams rankings held, in fact, two positions in the top fifteen: third with John Fitzgerald and fifteenth with Jacob Hlasek.

With such depth of talent to draw upon, it is not surprising that the 'miracle' manifests itself most markedly in recent Davis Cup results. When Sweden lost to Germany in December 1988, it was their sixth successive appearance in the final. In spite of the Germans having the highly regarded Boris Becker in their team, the depth of ability and experience in the Swedish side, playing on their home ground, had made the Scandinavians strong favourites. They had, in fact, won three of the previous five Davis Cup finals. By defeating Yugoslavia in the semi-final of the 1989 Davis Cup tournament, Sweden reached the final round for the seventh successive time. In December 1989 Sweden met Germany at Stuttgart. It is a rare occurrence for the same two countries to meet in successive years. West Germany came to the final with the confidence that goes with a run of eight successive Davis Cup victories and the undeniable strength of Boris Becker. Sweden, on the other hand, were out for revenge for the defeat in the previous final.

It was the first time for quite a few years that the Swedes were not the favourites to win. In Sweden, optimists took into consideration the talk of Boris Becker having suffered injuries, whereas pessimists were concerned over the lack of success in Wilander's game and even,

to a lesser extent, that of Edberg. The Swedes could well anticipate that a fit Becker, on a very fast home court, best designed to suit him, and in front of German supporters, would take a lot of beating in his two singles. Perhaps greatest concern was directed at the doubles partnership, on which the whole outcome could very likely depend. Järryd and Edberg had not recently reproduced their victories of previous years, having lost six of their twelve Davis Cup doubles partnerships together.

So Jonte Sjögren, the Davis Cup captain, was very much under scrutiny as far as selection and preparation were concerned. There had been quite a demand from various sources for a new partnership. Those who understood the subtler complications of the team structure, as far as singles alternatives were concerned, felt that, at the very least, Stefan and Anders needed much more Grand Prix standard practice together in doubles. Unfortunately, this highlights the conflicting considerations which are present when financial stakes are so high. They both have their personal interests in not playing doubles together. Stefan is concentrating on his singles ranking and keeping right at the top there, whilst Anders now plays happily and successfully with John Fitzgerald, with whom he won the Wimbledon title, and he bears in mind his chances of winning the Masters' doubles title. The top six Grand Prix doubles rankings compete for that title.

The Stockholm Open event gave the Swedish players and their Davis Cup captain the opportunity to assess various doubles combinations. Lundgren and Pernfors failed early on. Edberg partnered Wilander and they lost 6–4, 6–2 in the second round, albeit to the eventual winners Lozano and Witsken. Järryd played with Gunnarsson and they reached the third round before being defeated 6–3, 6–2 by the other eventual finalists, the Americans Leach and Pugh, who are at the very top of world rankings. At the subsequent press conference, the Davis Cup captain expressed his opinion that it was unfortunate that the opportunities for more matches with Järryd and Gunnarsson together had been cut short by meeting Leach and Pugh. He added, however, that the Americans' style of play was very different from that which the probable German doubles pair would present.

Jonte Sjögren went on to announce that the Swedish Davis Cup team would have at least ten days of doubles practice just prior to the meetings in Stuttgart and that there would be three centres arranged in Sweden with the opportunity to train on the same Pegulan surface that they would play on in Germany. He had three strong doubles combinations from which to choose, and not many countries were that fortunate.

In the first singles match of the Davis Cup Final, Mats Wilander had an almost four-and-a-half hour struggle to eventually triumph over Carl-Uwe Steeb. Germany levelled the score when Becker overwhelmed Edberg by 6–2, 6–2, 6–4. Then followed what was likely to be the decisive doubles match. Probably in the light of the deteriorating successes of the Edberg/Järryd combination and Stefan's heavy defeat in the singles, the team captain partnered Jan Gunnarsson with Anders. It was a long, five-set match in which Becker's power, especially when serving, was impressive. After being 6–7, 4–6 down, the Swedes fought back to level with 6–3, 7–6 and after four hours lost the deciding set 4–6. Critics may comment on Gunnarsson's lack of experience at that level and specify vital double-faults, but as 'Jonte' Sjögren pointed out, the Swedes actually won 169 points to the German's 163. In fact, it was so close that a net-ball going over instead of falling back, could have turned the tables.

The nearly eleven thousand supporters in Stuttgart were now prepared to will Becker to victory over Mats Wilander, the last hope for a Swedish 'miracle'. Any desperate hopes that the strenuous efforts of Boris in the doubles, while Mats had a rest day, might prove to be significant, were in vain. The strong young German crushed Wilander with an outstanding display of power tennis 6–2, 6–0, 6–2.

Just for the record. Edberg beat Steeb in the remaining match to produce a final result of 3–2. West Germany had won the Davis Cup in two successive years, having beaten Sweden in each of them. But the Swedish Davis Cup record is still impressive. Out of their last twenty-eight matches, the Swedes have lost only four. They have been beaten by one country other than Germany: they lost twice to Australia.

2 Tradition

Fifty years ago, Sweden did not figure very largely in the world of lawn tennis. The scene was dominated by players from the United States and Australia. A few European countries took it in turns to produce a star player and, in England, the recollection of the names of Fred Perry and Bunny Austin meant that the idea of an Englishman winning the men's singles title at Wimbledon had not yet become a dream with little real hope of fulfilment. In those days, cigarette packets contained picture cards which were keenly collected by youngsters. I remember Player's set of fifty Famous Tennis Players, but it did not contain a single Swede. Although, when asked for reasons to explain recent Swedish success, many Swedes include 'the long tradition of tennis in Sweden', I do not feel that this was all that widely known outside the rather small Swedish tennis fraternity itself.

When I first visited Sweden in 1949, with my own keen and active interest in tennis very much alive, I certainly did not get the impression of there being very much obvious interest, or activity, in the sport in Sweden, Båstad in those days was not very impressive, in international terms, and the Stockholm Open Tournament did not exist.

My own background experience in England had been of plenty of small tennis clubs where members turned up on the off-chance and the manipulation of some rota system determined with whom you played. Many of these clubs consisted of just two or three grass courts, and there was often as much of a social atmosphere about them as one of serious play. Most towns had a few public courts, even if the surfaces were not always up to a standard which one would have liked to have seen. The game was taught in schools, though mainly to girls. But there were usually courts of some kind or other, mostly on the same type of asphalt surfaces as school-playgrounds. In some schools these were available for boys too, if they were interested. Schools and colleges had fixtures and played matches against one another. Although the sport came in for the criticism, from time to time, of being an exclusive one and that a vast source of talent amongst youngsters from 'the lower social class' was not being tapped, I feel that this was rather exaggerated. Anyhow, I would certainly have expressed the opinion then, in the fifties, that tennis was a much more popular sport in England than in Sweden. Tennis in Sweden existed in the structural framework of local associations, just like many other sports. Yet we shall see in a later chapter that this could well be one of the most important contributory factors for subsequent success.

The climate is such in Sweden that grass courts do not exist. I do have a vague recollection of having seen a single grass court in the grounds of one of the smaller royal palaces, at Tullgarn. But it may have been a neglected and dilapidated old hard court. It was a relic from the days of King Gustav V's enthusiasm for the sport. Very recently there has been a proposal to repair and revive the first grass court that was created 120 years ago, in the grounds of a country estate in the province of Västergötland. It was on this court that the King used to play. But plans to develop an exclusive miniature Swedish 'Wimbledon', which could offer grass-court experience to top Swedish players, are still only in an early, optimistic stage.

It was King Gustav who really introduced and encouraged tennis in Sweden. After a visit to England in 1878–9, ostensibly in search of a suitable royal bride, he returned with a love of this sport which was little known in Sweden. During my first visit to Sweden, I bought a wooden carving of 'Mr G', as the King was affectionately known, especially in tennis circles. It was mass-produced and quite a crude caricature of the gangling, bespectacled monarch, clad in long trousers and wearing a hat. At that time one could hardly imagine a similar product, representing the British monarch, being marketed. But for the Swedes the image of a flannel-clad monarch carrying a tennis racket was a popular one.

As far as I could determine, there were no tennis clubs in the early fifties as I had known them. Nor were there many, if any, public courts available. Those clubs that did exist were of the type where a membership sub-scription entitled the members to book a court at a specific time with their own partners and/or opponents. It was not a club for a social gath-ering, in the sense then common in England. These courts were of the En-Tout-Cas variety and I did see a few inflated covered courts, in addition to a small number of permanently built tennis-halls in the larger towns.

There has never been anything like the same amount of inter-collegiate sporting events in Sweden as there has been in Britain and the United States. Even less so, has it been the case

King Gustaf of Sweden playing at Nice in the 1920s.

in Swedish schools. Tennis was no exception to this traditional state of affairs, and was probably featured even less than other sports in which there may have been the odd inter-institutional fixture.

As far as tennis was concerned, as in many other areas, Sweden was a late developer. As a nation, Sweden has for some few decades now been held up as an example of modern progress and attitudes. Neutrality during World War Two left Sweden in a relatively affluent position which it has managed to maintain. Yet it is not so very long ago that Sweden was a poor country from which hundreds of thousands of people emigrated to escape from the rigours and poverty of their homeland. There are nowadays almost as many descendants of these emigrants living in the US as the eight million or so who live in Sweden itself. The Industrial Revolution came late to Sweden. But this was not only a negative thing. Sweden gained many advantages from its later start. It could learn from the mistakes of others. There is, for example, no equivalent of the slums which sprang up in the industrial towns of Britain. The capital, unlike many others in Europe, did not have an underground railway system until 1950. But, before constructing the Tunnelbana in Stockholm, the Swedes were able to visit the London Underground network, the Paris Metro and equivalent systems in Berlin and Moscow, to select the good features that were appropriate to Swedish needs and avoid many of the mistakes which had become apparent elsewhere. Even in the case of traffic, Sweden was the last mainland country of Europe to adopt a system of driving on the right-hand side of the road, doing so in 1967.

My general impression is that when the Swedes decide to undertake anything they expect a good quality result; they are thorough and well-organized in their preparation and determined in their striving. These same qualities, which I observed at first-hand in that incredibly successful handling of the complicated traffic change-over operation, are present in the tennis success story.

This late start, which gathers momentum to produce a good final product, is exemplifed in other sports, too. The first football matches which I watched in Sweden struck me as being very amateurish and of quite a poor standard. Yet before many more years had passed, the national side was doing well in the World Cup. Very little golf was played in Sweden thirty, forty years ago and there were certainly very few names of Swedish golfers known outside Scandinavia. But that sport has boomed and flourished tremendously in recent years. It is not impossible to imagine that within the next decade there could be a story of international achievement with Swedish successes in golf that equal, or even surpass, what has happened in Swedish tennis. It might be interesting to know what parallels there are between the possible explanations of success in these two ball-games in this country where climatic conditions would certainly appear to be a considerable disadvantage compared to that of the more traditionally successful lands. In table-tennis, as well, the Swedes have recently achieved great international success. In April 1989 they broke the long Chinese domination of the sport by winning the world team title and the men's singles title.

Svenska Tennisförbundet (STF), the Swedish Tennis Association, had its very insignifcant beginnings in 1906. Swedish Tennis was struck a considerable blow when in 1915 its main tennis-hall near the Stadium, in Stockholm, was destroyed by fire. It is possibly a reflection of the real lack of interest and support that it was more than two decades before the sport regained its own identifiable central gathering point. It was not until King Gustav V donated the sum of 50,000 kronor, on the occasion of his eightieth birthday, that a new home for tennis became a reality. That was in 1938. This new Kungliga Tennishallen (Royal Covered Tennis Courts) then attracted financial support from some leading Swedish businessmen.

This was not the first help that Mr G had given to Swedish tennis. The story is told of him playing on the old cement courts in Båstad, in 1930. A tumble resulted in the monarch scraping his knuckles. The following season Båstad could boast of a fine clay court replacement.

In 1925 Sweden entered the Davis Cup competition, which had started a quarter of a century earlier, for the first time. They beat Switzerland, in Bern. One of the good young Swedish competitors was Marcus Wallenberg. The Wallenbergs were, and are, a very wealthy family of bankers. The financial support which the Wallenbergs have given to Swedish tennis must have had a strong impact on the development of the sport. Of course, money is not the be-all and end-all, but it helps. This was long before the rather more investment-type of financial support given in the form of sponsorships today, with advertising very much in mind.

Another member of the first Swedish Davis Cup team was Sune Malmström. He came close to beating the legendary Jean Borotra in the 1926 match against France. But Swedish international standing was still very much limited to the odd flash in the pan.

It was the exploits of Kalle Schröder that first really made the name of a Swedish tennis player internationally known and raised the reputation of Swedish tennis to a level that it had not known before. At the age of twenty he defeated the famous Borotra in the Indoor Championships in Paris. But his inability to master top European players on outdoor courts resulted in Kalle never reaching the heights of overall world ranking.

There can be little doubt that Kalle Schröder was the first to lead the way towards high standards in Swedish tennis. He was the first really good player and outstandingly so in pre-war years. He became a professional and continued to make his contribution to the sport as coach at KLTK, the Royal Lawn Tennis Club.

The Stockholm Open Tournament was held from 1969 to 1988 in Kungliga Tennishallen (Royal Covered Tennis Courts) where the bust of Mr G is a reminder of the Swedish monarch's influence on the sport. In those twenty years the Open men's singles title has been won by fourteen different players, from seven different countries. No less than eight winners of the Stockholm Open have won Grand Slam titles and six have been Wimbledon victors. Players from the United States have been the most successful in winning the singles tournament so far, with a total of eleven. It was not until 1980 that a Swede won, when Björn Borg beat John McEnroe 6–3, 6–4. But since then Mats Wilander has won in 1983 and Stefan Edberg in both 1986 and 1987.

It was during the forties and fifties that play on the Royal Courts gradually made its influence felt on this developing sport. A further reflection of Mr G's contribution was Kungens kanna (the King's Trophy). Introduced eighty years ago, the King's Trophy gained in international reputation and attraction in the post-war years. Lennart Bergelin became a hero, at least within his own country, when he defeated the well-known Jaroslav Drobny, the Czechoslovak who won Wimbledon in 1954. This was also the third successive time that

Bergelin had won the King's Trophy.

If Kalle Schröder may be said to have laid the foundations for the popularity of tennis in Sweden in the thirties, then one must also recognize the importance of what happened in 1946 to open up a new era. The venue was at Varberg, a Swedish coastal town south of Göteborg (Gothenburg). The deciding Davis Cup match was to be fought out between Bergelin and Yugoslavia's Dragutin Mitic. It went to five sets and the fifth was a long-setter. Not before 10–8 did Bergelin and Sweden win. Pulling back from having been two sets down was a remarkable performance and it became known, as it is still today, as the miracle at Varberg.

The fact that Sweden was whitewashed by the US 5–0 in the interzonal final did little to diminish the Swedish pride at the achievement in Varberg Swedish tennis had been put on the map. With the combination of good players and the new confidence to go with them, it became a not uncommon occurrence for Sweden to win the European zone of the Davis Cup. Four years later they won again and followed up that victory the very next year. The years 1954, 1962 and 1964 saw Swedish successes in the European section, only to be frustrated in the interzonal final. It was nearly thirty years before Sweden was to go further in the Davis Cup than Lennart Bergelin and Torsten Johansson had taken them at Varberg.

Undoubtedly, the present-day strength of Swedish Davis Cup successes lies in the depth of the country's tennis talent. After Varberg, Bergelin and Johansson bore the brunt alone. Torsten never achieved great heights in international tournaments, athough the record books show an amazing set of figures from the Wimbledon of 1947. He won his first six singles sets without losing a game. Torsten was the

solid, reliable player in the Swedish Davis Cup team for many years. He won more than 70 per cent of the nearly fifty singles matches in which he represented his country. He has gone on achieving national titles as a veteran in a remarkable way. As a sixty-six-year-old he won the Swedish Veterans' title yet again. That victory brought the total of his Swedish championship titles to no less than seventy! Then he had only lost once since its inception in 1972. But he did lose in the doubles in 1988. He is reported as saying that he had lost before, but he couldn't remember when. By now he is

Lennart Bergelin, coach, mentor and friend to Björn Borg.

nearing his hundredth title in Swedish veteran championships.

Lennart Bergelin, however, did have more noticeable successes in international tournaments. He reached the last eight at Wimbledon in the men's singles in 1948.

Lennart Bergelin and Torsten Johansson alone formed the Swedish Davis Cup team until 1950, when they were joined by a young player named Sven Davidson. His début was in the doubles match against Australia when, together with Bergelin, the Swedes lost in three straight sets. But Davidson was destined to go on to better things and to become generally regarded as the greatest Swedish tennis-player, up until the advent of the fabulous Björn Borg.

Sven had already won his first King's Trophy in his twentieth year, in 1948. Two years later he won three titles in the French Indoor Championships. He did better than any Swede had previously done in the US Championships at Forest Hills when he lost 9–11 in the fifth set of the semi-finals to the Australian Ken Rosewall. In 1954 he became the first Swede to win the US Indoor Championship. Then the following year came his first Grand Slam final. It was in the French Open, in Paris, that Sven reached the final, to be beaten by the American Tony Trabert. Two years later in 1957 he became the first Swede to win a Grand Slam title when he beat the American Herb Flam in three straight sets in the final in Paris. This was crowned by a doubles victory at Wimbledon, the following year, in partnership with Ulf Schmidt, a fellow Swede.

Without a doubt, Sven Davidson must be considered as the Swedish tennis-player to have achieved the best results before Björn Borg and the subsequent successful stream of young players:

Sven Davidson, who now lives in the US, considers the three most important factors contributing to Sweden's success in tennis to be Björn Borg, the coming of open tennis and the big prize-money. Borg's phenomenal success, bringing fame and riches, not only provided an idealistic inspiration, but showed a way to what Sven has described as 'big net income outside of the punishing Swedish tax system'. Of the twenty leading Swedish male players, only nine give their residence as Sweden, whilst there are six in Monte Carlo, three in the US, and two in Britain.

Ulf Schmidt was Sven Davidson's partner in the first Swedish Wimbledon victory, and he was a worthy player in his own right. In a period of ten years from the middle of the fifties he played no fewer than 102 Davis Cup matches, a feat surpassed by very few. In 1956 he became the youngest man to win the US Indoor Championship. The final was an all-Swedish event, as it was Sven Davidson who was beaten. Ulf repeated this win over Sven by beating him in the Båstad Championship.

In 1959 Schmidt made his first Davis Cup appearance. For six years, he and Jan-Erik Lundqvist together made a big contribution to Swedish Davis Cup tennis. Jan-Erik Lundqvist was never able to achieve the same impressive results as Bergelin or Davidson, or even Ulf Schmidt's Wimbledon title, but he is well remembered by those who saw him play and who appreciate the artistry of the game of tennis. He now runs a private tennis-centre in Stockholm.

But there is another person to whom Sweden, undoubtedly, owes a great deal for the successes they have gained. Yet strangely enough I have only come across the name of Bill Lufler in one written attempt, amongst Swedish writers, to account for the development of the sport. William Lufler was an American coach. He did not achieve great results as a player, but enjoyed a very good reputation as a coach. He is an outstanding example of the financial support which the Wallenbergs provided. At the very end of the forties, the Swedish Tennis Association realized the need for a good national coach. Wallenberg wanted to know who was considered to be the best and what it would cost to obtain his services. When he was satisfied that the suggested William Lufler was what Swedish tennis needed, he offered the money needed to secure him for the next five years.

As well as his work with junior tennis-players, Lufler concentrated on developing a coaching corps. He travelled widely throughout Sweden and attended courses arranged by area associations, for which the STF bore the expenses. Lufler took groups of instructors and young juniors. He went through his coaching stroke by stroke with the instructors and then they immediately endeavoured to put their more or less theoretical knowledge into practice with the youngsters. Lufler was especially keen to promote attacking tennis. He emphasized volley play and a novel form of top spin in backhand strokes. Lufler's ideas were regarded as new and brilliant. He brought a

personal encouragement to continued efforts within the associations.

One of the instructors trained by Lufler, and subsequently his assistant, was Percy Rosberg, a key figure today in Swedish tennis. Percy first discovered and developed the young Björn Borg when he came from Södertälje to the Stockholm Tennis Club (SALK). He also coached Stefan Edberg in his earlier years.

Another manifestation of Lufler's continuing influence on Swedish tennis is through Jonte Sjögren. He came under the American coach's influence at a training camp for juniors. In typical Lufler style, Jonte found himself assisting Lufler in the coaching of other youngsters. Sjögren went on to become Swedish Junior Champion in 1956, and the peak of his personal achievements was probably that of reaching the final of the Swedish Outdoor Championships in 1963, when he lost to Janne Lundqvist. Sjögren has had, in his turn, as coach and captain, an enormous influence on Sweden's Davis Cup successes.

But it was not until 1972, when a fifteen-year-old made his first appearance in the Swedish Davis Cup side, that the first hopeful signs of the reputation of Swedish tennis being lifted out of the doldrums came about. That fifteen-year-old was, of course, Björn Borg.

3 The Swedish system of sports associations

The Swedish Sports Federation (SSF) has been in existence for nearly ninety years. Its early beginnings tended to be associated with pastimes for the wealthier members of the population, but it has developed, with ever increasing acceleration, into the country's largest popular movement. Almost a third of all Swedes are involved in one or more sporting or recreational activities.

Sweden is divided into twenty-three administrative districts. For the last two decades, the SSF has been active in all of them. There are nearly sixty different sports associations in this federation and since 1906 the Swedish Tennis Association (STF) has been one of them. All the regional offices of these various sports are well supplied with staff and finances in order to serve the associations in a variety of ways. These include many different sorts of courses: some are administrative and others are intended for coaches, trainers, leaders, referees and umpires, etc.

In the case of the STF it is estimated that somewhere between 250,000 and 300,000 people play tennis more or less regularly. Of those, more than 130,000 are registered members of about 950 clubs affiliated to the Association. These clubs vary in size, from the very small with not more than fifteen members up to the Uppsala Tennis Club, the largest, with nearly 3,000 members. About one-sixth of the STF registered membership is made up of juniors, with about three boys for every girl. Probably 50–60 per cent of these clubs have reasonably good development programmes for juniors, led by amateur trainers who have taken the Stage 1 or Stage 2 courses offered by the STF. Sometimes the more talented juniors move on to another club which is able to offer better opportunities than the more limited original club. Birger Folke, Swedish Davis Cup captain 1967–9, considers that 200 of these clubs work professionally and have a really good programme.

The STF and the Regional Associations organize a very full programme of tournaments and competitions. Jeremy Bates, Britain's number one men's singles player, has compared British tennis with conditions in Sweden: 'When people have leisure time they are able to play on indoor courts, of which there are plenty. I've been in the clubs in Sweden and they're running leagues for all age groups, every day of the week, all through the summer and all through the winter. The whole thing is in just a completely different dimension from what it is in the UK. The average club in England possibly only runs one tournament a year.'

A tournament of particular value to Swedish tennis is the Donald Duck Tournament (or Kalle Anka, as he is called in Swedish). This competition, sponsored by the Walt Disney organization, started in Sweden in 1969. It has been a tremendous success and has now been started in other countries, where it is called The Goofy Cup. There are as many as 13,000 entrants each year. Boys and girls participate

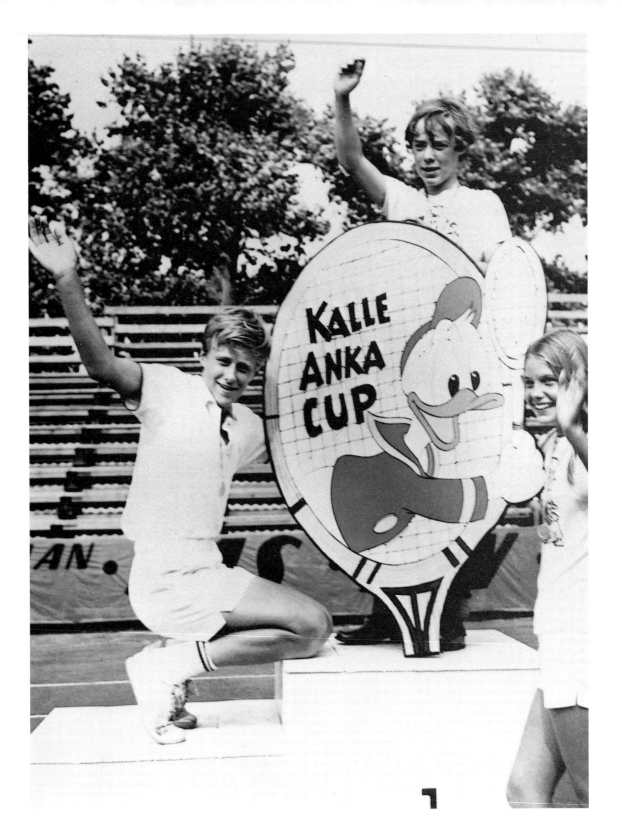

KALLE ANKA CUP

1

in three age classes of eleven, thirteen and fifteen years. Since the raising of the lower age limit in national and international tournaments, the eleven-year-class remains in the Kalle Anka tournament, but not on a knock-out basis.

From each of the twenty-three local district tournaments, one winner goes forward into each section of the competition. These finalists then meet for the major tournament held in Båstad. It is here that many promising young players first make their mark. For example, Mats Wilander won his first Donald Duck triumph there, as an eleven-year-old. In fact, Mikael Pernfors is probably the only recent top-ranking Swedish player who has not first made his name at the Kalle Anka tournament. He spent his formative years in the US.

Competitions for young players rank highly in Ove Bengtsson's list of things which have helped to raise the standard of Swedish tennis so much. Ove was a mainstay of Swedish Davis Cup teams from 1967 to 1979. His comment, 'It stimulates "replacement-growth"' sounds rather stuffy, when translated from Swedish, but it is a very accurate description of just what these competitions do. Birger Folke makes the comment, 'The best ones have to be very good to go through the tournaments.'

In discussing the organization of the Association and the clubs, Carl-Axel Hageskog (the Swedish Davis Cup team coach) has used the term 'vacuum cleaner' in an analogy to describe how the whole of Sweden is searched for talented beginners. 'All (or almost all) are discovered if they are good,' he claims.

Ove Bengtsson also considers the unified system of educating tennis trainers, throughout the length and breadth of the country, as being one of the major contributory factors to Swedish success. Carl-Axel Hageskog, too, is full of praise for the voluntary work done in the clubs and he shares Ove's opinion concerning the contribution made by the good system of training coaches.

The Swedish Tennis Instructors Association is a newly formed association. In February 1988 there were 211 members of which 90 were full-time trainers and sixty were part-time. The remainder were basically unpaid. Only eleven were women. The latest figures, at May 1989, show a membership increase of about 17 per cent.

In Sweden there is a three-stage system of qualification for tennis instructors. There is no written or oral examination at any level; regular attendance at the courses is sufficient. The Stage 1 and Stage 2 courses are of only fourteen-and-a-half and fourteen hours total duration respectively, but the higher Stage 3 is for forty-four-and-a-half hours. In addition there is a range of specialist courses which average around twelve hours. During a recent ten-year period, some 7–8,000 people have gone through the Stage 1 and Stage 2 courses.

There are plans to introduce a Stage 4, but at the present time the only higher qualification is through attendance at the Swedish Physical Training College. Entrance to these two-year courses is extremely limited and the successful participants emerge as qualified Physical Education teachers and also skilled tennis trainers. There are not more than about twenty tennis clubs in Sweden with sufficient membership to support a full-time professional.

Each of the regional tennis associations has a

Young Borg with other competitors in the Donald Duck Tournament.

junior leader. He usually co-operates with a few of the best trainers in the region to provide weekend training camps for the top thirteen- to fourteen-year-olds, up to about four times a year.

In addition to the twenty-three administrative regions, the STF has created six 'super-regions'. These arrange weekend gatherings similar to the regional training camps, but they are at a somewhat higher level and have to be restricted to about a dozen participants. These events are given financial support by the STF.

There is also the annual gathering of the very top fourteen-year-old boys and girls at what has become known as the Davis Cup School. About sixty boys and girls are split into groups and are given intensive training on and off the court for six days. This is regarded as being the best tennis coaching that is available in Sweden. It is held in Båstad and Percy Rosberg has been the inspiring force there for many years.

Also held in Båstad, in the same month of May, is the annual Élite Training Camp, to which no more than thirty of the best fourteen- to eighteen-year-old boys and girls are invited. It is from this élite group that selections are made for national representational honours. All the top leaders, coaches and trainers attend this gathering.

Most of the work done in these sports associations is by volunteers. Although in some cases the growing size of membership results in standards falling short of the ideal, there is little doubt that the co-operative effort and involvement create an all-important *esprit* that contributes towards success.

The idea of the amateur trainer is widespread throughout Swedish sport. Most of the sports associated with the Swedish Sports Federation offer courses to encourage club members who wish to teach their sport to beginners and intermediates. There is financial support and encouragement from the communities for these courses, but often the actual teaching is then quite unpaid. It may eventually lead on to work on a semi-professional basis (and, of course, there are full professionals as well) but the majority remain as amateurs.

But, obviously, Swedish sport does not rely on volunteers and enthusiasm alone. A lot of money is needed to support such active programmes.

All junior programmes in Swedish clubs, for beginners or advanced juniors, enjoy funding from government and the local community to which the club belongs. To obtain this help one has to have one trainer and five pupils. This financial support has now been available for fifteen years or more and has become a highly valued contribution to all sports.

In 1987–8 the Swedish State paid 256m kronor (about £25m) to the National Sports Association. Of this amount, 3.5m kronor (about £350,000) went to the Swedish Tennis Association.

The equivalent of county councils paid 100m kronor (about £10m) to the twenty-three regional sports organizations. Of this sum, the regional tennis associations received an estimated 2m kronor (about £200,000).

Local government authorities donated more than 3,500m kronor (about £350m) to sports clubs (which number about 40,000 throughout the country) of which 2.5 billion was to support building facilities, such as ice-hockey rinks, tennis-halls, etc. and the remaining 1 billion for running expenses.

In addition, the clubs get a direct grant from the state, via the National Sports Association, of 80m kronor (about £8m) for running expenses.

As far as tennis was concerned, the STF, as one of fifty-seven sports associations, received about one-seventieth of the state grant. This formed about a quarter of the total STF budget.

Apart from these state grants, other important sources of income arise from the Davis Cup and other tournaments. A successful run in the Davis Cup brings considerable revenue, as well as national prestige. There is also income from radio and television and the testing and approving of tennis equipment. Moving the Stockholm Open tournament from The Royal Courts to the new, splendid Globe stadium will increase the possible spectator capacity from about 4,000 to 14,000. At the same time, the average cost of seats has fallen by nearly 30 per cent. The organizers have been hoping for a profit of around half a million dollars, much of which will go directly or indirectly to benefit the tennis clubs. This profit is in spite of the greatly increased prize money offered to attract the top players. The prizes of more than a million dollars at the Stockholm Open now rank amongst the very highest after the four Grand Slam events.

There was great jubilation and some relief, towards the end of 1987, when a sponsorship of around £2m, over a five-year period, was promised by Beckers, a large company which is mainly involved in paint products.

The former champion Jan-Erik Lundqvist sums it up succinctly: 'In my opinion the Swedish Tennis Wonder is fairly logical. It is obviously important to have a well-functioning association, competent trainers, a good number of courts and a background tradition. These we have in Sweden.'

4 Playing facilities

Few people involved in Swedish tennis consider the coaching situation to be a great problem, in spite of the fact that their reputation for success has made coaches from Sweden highly attractive exports, especially to the US and Germany. At least fifty trainers have been attracted overseas. In Austria, a tennis training centre has been established called Die Schwedische Tennisschule (the Swedish Tennis School). The coaches, who vary in number seasonally from five to eight, are all qualified Swedish tennis coaches.

But the almost unanimous cry is for yet more courts! After Björn Borg's victories such a lot of young boys were attracted to the clubs that there are really still too many applicants for the clubs to accommodate. There are waiting lists for entry to almost every club. In the early part of 1987, in spite of a ratio of indoor courts to players which compares most favourably with the vast majority of countries, the theoretical availability of a free court to each member of the STF was an hour once a fortnight.

Björn Borg's success acted as a stimulant to the amount of interest in playing tennis, and led to the subsequent building of courts, including indoor courts. The authorities in communities throughout Sweden began to take tennis more seriously and regard it as a 'legitimate' popular sport.

There has been a tremendous boom in indoor tennis facilities in recent years across the country. In *Tennis Tidningen*, the monthly magazine issued by the Swedish Tennis Association, there have been regular articles for several years that feature one or two of the latest of such constructions, and giving considerable details about the fund raising. The STF has also produced a series of leaflets which give information about recent achievements in statistical form and provide practical advice for clubs and communities considering undertaking such projects.

These show that in 1985 there were thirty-two newly built tennis-halls with 72 courts. Seventeen more followed in 1986 with 49 courts; 1987 provided a further thirteen halls with 39 courts and in 1988 a highly successful year for tennis in Sweden, yet another fifteen halls with 54 courts. Thus, in a period of four years there were seventy-seven new tennis-halls built throughout the country which provided more than 200 new courts. By 1 March 1988 this had brought the number of courts in tennis-halls to a total of 560, an increase of about 60 per cent over those four years.

That figure of 560 courts represents two-thirds of a court for every 10,000 inhabitants. There is still a considerable regional variation in availability and the number of courts per 10,000 people varies between 0.1 and 1.3. More than 200 of the available courts are in the ten largest centres of population, with nearly a hundred in Stockholm.

The Swedish Tennis Association aims to have 250,000 club members by 1995, with a further quarter of a million playing tennis in a less formalized way. To achieve this they calculate that they will need to provide yet another 320 new courts, and so alter the present figure of a court for every 15,000 inhabitants to that of 9,000.

However, in spite of this tremendous boom in the provision of indoor tennis facilities, which was required and demanded by the tremendous growth in popularity of the sport, official statistics show that outdoor courts still account for as many as 82 per cent of those in Sweden, being more or less equally divided between clay and asphalt surfaces. It should not be forgotten that during normal climatic conditions in much of the country there is little more than the three-month season of June, July and August for outdoor play. Even in the southern areas there is hardly any more extra playing time than May and the first half of September.

A check on the numbers of covered courts shows that in the middle of 1986 the 55 million British had 189 whilst 8 million Swedes had 1,200. On a per capita basis, this works out to be about forty-four times as many.

Jeremy Bates has described coming out of school at 4 o'clock on a winter's afternoon, when it gets dark almost immediately afterwards: 'Living in Birmingham, supposedly the second city in the UK, there weren't any indoor courts where I could play. Nor was there anyone of good standard with whom I could practise. This is where we are so far behind.' Compare this to Jonas Svensson: 'Everybody in Sweden is able to play tennis. The clubs are alive, due to good junior programmes. The juniors always get the best court-times, after school.'

In September 1989 a quotation from Warren Jacques, Britain's national team coach, appeared in Swedish, saying, 'One of the reasons for England's poor recovery is that the courts in Britain are worthless.' This followed

Mini-tennis, fun for children and a good opportunity to spot talent and to cultivate it.

an earlier prediction that Britain would have six players in the men's top fifty rankings within the next five years.

Janne Lundqvist has commented: 'Most important is the fact that tennis in Sweden is very popular. This means that boys of the right potential (the so-called "hungry guys") come to tennis. The competition is very strong; almost as strong as in Australia during the fifties and sixties, when Harry Hopman was in charge. I believe this not to be the case in England, France, Spain and Italy, for example, where other sports are the main attraction and it seems as though only the "non-qualifying" youngsters go into tennis. Perhaps this is even more obvious in the USA where one finds hundreds of super stars in almost every sport . . . except tennis, where there are plenty of average and above-average players but few real "super-stars". Continental tennis seems to be a social game where people go to the clubs in the spirit of having a good game, have a drink in the bar and meet friends. With few exceptions, alcohol is not served in Swedish tennis clubs and the courts are open to the public.'

Sven Davidson, the former Swedish champion, sums it up thus: 'I refuse to believe that Swedes have more "talent" than anybody else. Britain has a population about seven times that of Sweden. If seven times more British boys than Swedish boys would try out the game, year in and year out, you would have many new Fred Perrys. I fear, however, that only one-seventh of the number of boys in Sweden get a chance in tennis in Britain. The organization of Swedish tennis is reasonably good, which means that anyone who wants to can get a chance to try out the game.'

5 Solving the problem of education

Since the days when there was quite an uproar over the young Björn Borg deciding to forsake his schooling and concentrate entirely on a future as a professional tennis player, there have been many attempts to deal satisfactorily with the problems which such a decision obviously involves. Even for those who succeed in their tennis careers and achieve the highest rankings and the greatest financial rewards, there are attendant problems and sacrifices which have had to be made. For every success story there are hundreds, even thousands, of others who do not achieve such pinnacles. As in the majority of careers, one does not really know what the job involves until one is embarked upon it. When young players give up continued formal education to concentrate on playing tennis for their future livelihood, only to find that they cannot continue with the life-style which this demands, or do not have the full ability required, or are struck down by injury, they may well regret they did not continue their schooling.

In Sweden, various attempts have been made to overcome or minimize this problem and there are still several alternatives which the individual youngster considering a future as a professional tennis player may take. One of them is the Båstad Tennis School, situated in the small coastal resort in the southernmost Swedish province and often referred to as Sweden's tennis Mecca.

At the Båstad Tennis School, the Swedish Tennis Association has been able to arrange for training at the highest level combined with continued formal schooling at an adult education college within walking distance of its indoor and outdoor courts. Such colleges, known as Kom Vux, are widespread throughout the country and normally provide part-time or full-time educational courses for those over the age of eighteen years. In the case of Båstad Tennis School, the legislation has been altered to admit even slightly younger students and the courses are so arranged that the day's programmes are divided between tennis and formal education; the duration of the courses is extended beyond that usually needed to allow for this and also to make it possible for the young players to travel away to participate in appropriate tournaments world-wide. Additionally, the courses are flexible so that the individual can devote even more time to tennis or revert to academic studies, if that seems to be the wiser decision.

Båstad Tennis School has been known internationally as the Swedish National Tennis Centre. Since 1 July 1989 Tretorn, the leading Swedish manufacturers of tennis-balls, have sponsored some of the activities at the School and it is now referred to as Tretorn Tennis Academy. Students there are entitled to the same educational grants for studies, accommodation and home-travel as other students attending secondary schools.

The first group of fourteen students, seven of each sex, started the course in the 1985–6 academic year. They were required to have

The finals of the Donald Duck Tournament are inaugurated with a ceremony on the centre court at Båstad.

above average playing ability, the aim of becoming professional tennis players, adequate school qualifications to entitle them to attend the normal Kom Vux courses and to sign a contract as a player with the Tennis Association.

In addition to the academic courses, the young tennis players train for about three hours each weekday, and do a certain amount of training during the weekend. They also have other physical training more or less every other day. A wide range of training relevant to their chosen career is provided and this includes both physical and mental aspects of the game.

The individualizing of the programme depends on the student's physical condition and what is felt by the player and his coaches to be appropriate to his, or her, current needs. The weekly programme may range from no tennis training at all, together with a couple of light physical training sessions, up to nine training sessions, totalling thirteen-and-a-half hours, plus two physical training sessions. A typical twelve-week period for a player may include five weeks of tournament play, divided into two parts, interspersed by training.

Players have a choice of eight training themes, the timing and order of selection depending on individual circumstances and choice:

1 Technique: when time is devoted to attain the optimal results with each player as an individual. The use of ball-machines plays an important role in this respect.

2 Mobility: great stress is placed on this; it is described as possibly the most important theme.

3 Return of service: with concentration on accuracy, sureness, spin and ball-speed.

4 Offensive play: on the assumption that the typical 'Swedish style' of safe baseline has already been well established in the young player, time is here devoted to the more attacking aspects of play.

5 Tempo: which does not only mean hard hitting and quick moving, but refers more to taking the ball early and thereby putting pressure on the opponent. It also encompasses placing and anticipation.

6 Playing for the point: involves purposeful play to win the point, albeit possibly under the training of some special tactical approach. This is intensified before tournament play periods.

7 Doubles: both with a specific partner in preparation for competitive play or purely for training in the patterns of that form of the game.

8 Physical training with racket and ball: to increase speed, strength, condition and endurance.

In addition to these eight themes, students are taught how to cope with the life of a professional tennis-player. There is advice on diet, on how to avoid and recover from injuries, on massage, and such basics as shoes, strings, rackets, etc. Mental training is integrated into the course, under the guidance of Lars Ryberg, a sports psychologist, and tailored to individual requirements.

Everything is done to smooth the path for the young competitors and whenever possible one of the trainers accompanies them to appropriate tournaments.

Established players are welcome to return and train with the resident students for varying periods of time. Many have already done so. Although this is encouraged, it is not allowed to be to the detriment of the students undertaking the main course.

The Tretorn Tennis Academy now boasts an attractive main hall which encloses three courts. Five new outdoor courts are in the process of being added to the original nine. Two of the fourteen courts are Plexipave. With the unusually mild climate of Båstad, sheltered in the lee of the Halland Ridge, the courts are ready for play by the end of March. Now another hall is planned with two or three tennis courts.

Not surprisingly, not everyone is enthusiastic about the Tennis School in Båstad. Tim Klein is a German immigrant to Sweden who has established a strong reputation for his successes with several good Swedish players in the Team Tim Klein, which includes Jonas Svensson and the great up-setter at the Stockholm Open, Magnus Gustafsson. Tim is known for being outspoken and reactions to him are extreme, both positively and negatively. After his sensational successes in the Stockholm Open, Magnus stated that Tim Klein was responsible for 50 per cent of his tennis. He dismisses the type of training in Båstad as being a protected workshop and not the sort of place where top players can be trained. Tony Pickard, Stefan Edberg's coach, has made similar criticisms.

Bengt Cronvall, Director of Tretorn Tennis Academy, stresses that Båstad is only one of the alternatives available and that it may not be the ideal solution for all young aspiring players. There is, for example, the regional Tennis High School in Vetlanda, where Birger Andersson is the chief instructor. There is also the alternative of staying at the normal school nearest to home and being allowed five lesson periods a week to concentrate on a specific sport. Currently there are only about twenty such places available for tennis throughout the country. The choice between backing everything on a 'tennis only' future as opposed to the tennis/studies combination, is not an easy one. The young player must be advised to consider not only Mats Wilander's opinion that it is highly improbable that one can combine reaching the top of the world rankings with studies, but also the scores of examples of those who did not succeed sufficiently well, even with such concentration on their sport.

One of Båstad's current successes is the eighteen-year-old Niklas Kulti, the winner of the 1989 Junior Wimbledon's men's singles title and World Junior Champion. As a fourteen-year-old the young Niklas signed a contract for £100,000. It is interesting to note that this amount is twenty times greater than Björn Borg's first contract, with SAS, as a seventeen-year-old, in 1973. Not surprisingly, there has been a lot of criticism from some sources about this kind of transaction at such an early age. However, Per Bergentoft, an instructor at the School and also the physiotherapist for the Davis Cup team, thinks that the contract has made Niklas a better player.

Thus this School in Båstad, called by whatever name, is certainly a most interesting and successful attempt to solve the dilemma which faces young people who are seriously considering becoming professional players and who appear to have the necessary attributes. It is no wonder then that Bengt Cronvall reports an ever-increasing number of expressions of interest in the work that is currently going on, from many parts of the world, and from official sources requesting to visit. It is reported that there are between 100,000 and 120,000 visitors annually to the sports complex at Drivan.

Schools of a similar type are becoming more and more common in other parts of the world. Each country tries the format which seems best to suit their individual educational systems and the funding available. It is very much a matter of trial and error, to try to combine the best possible tennis training opportunities with the chance to continue a more formal education. The latter has the dual purpose of developing a full personality player not continuing with a tennis career.

A very different alternative that many young Swedes have tried is the American college

Niklas Kulti, 1989 World Junior Champion.

scholarship. The success of Swedish tennis has created great interest in Swedish players and the number at American colleges is now approaching two hundred. Mikael Pernfors has been instrumental in focusing attention on this possibility, as he is the shining example of success obtained through this method, which additionally offers the easy absorption of the English language, an inexpensive university education and broadening of the mind associated with foreign travel.

Britain has the Lawn Tennis Association School at Bisham Abbey, in Buckinghamshire, which was started in 1983 and is for boys only. They number around a dozen. The School is structured to provide a unique combination of conventional scholastic education with specialized tennis coaching and training in a residential environment. The facilities provided for tennis are excellent. Perhaps the most striking difference, compared with the Swedish version in Båstad, quite apart from the single-sex and younger entry at fourteen plus, is that normal schooling comes in the middle part of the day. There is early morning physical activity before attending classes in a local school. Playing practice during the week is concentrated into the early evening. There are good facilities for physical fitness programmes at Bisham Abbey and there is also a psychological skills programme. Those who are keen to see a revival of British tennis will be watching eagerly for the achievements of the young players emerging from this attempt to provide a 'normal' education with concentrated tennis coaching.

Another new path, now open to young players in Britain, is that of the YTA (Youth Training Scheme). Some players have already taken advantage of this method of obtaining training and in a few cases it has led to the early stages of success. Instead of requiring parents to meet the not inconsiderable expenses involved with equipment, travelling, accommodation, etc., the YTA scheme pays wages and provides help with accommodation expenses.

6 Minitennis

Minitennis is in no way unique to Sweden, for various adaptations of the game have been made to make it easier for beginners, especially for younger players. In Britain it is known as 'short tennis'. But it is probably longer established and more extensively integrated into training programmes in Sweden than in other countries.

The British Lawn Tennis Association has produced a video cassette on 'short tennis' and did, in fact, do so before the Swedish Tennis Association came out recently with their video on minitennis. There was good-humoured teasing about this fact, between the associations, as minitennis has been in operation in Sweden for nearly twenty years now.

The Nytell brothers, Hans and Ulf, are regarded as the leading authorities on minitennis in Sweden. They introduced a minitennis school at the Uppsala Tennis Club (UTK) more than sixteen years ago. UTK is the largest tennis club in Sweden, with more than 4,000 members and is open to all ages and levels of players. Consequently, minitennis finds an obvious and successful place in the club's existence.

It cannot be stressed too much that the main aim of minitennis is for it to be fun.

In this adapted form, the court, the racket and the balls are suited to the stage of development of the beginner. It is particularly suitable for children in the age-range of seven to nine years, though some six-year-olds and even younger can cope.

Minitennis can be played on most surfaces and is equally suitable indoors or outdoors. In Sweden, it now tends to be mostly organized in tennis-halls. On a normal-sized tennis court, there is room to mark out four minitennis courts. This quadruples the amount of coaching volume possible, compared with attempting to play on a full-size court. The net is used at a central height of 80cm (as compared with the regulation height of 91cm at the centre and 107cm at the sides, of a full-size court). Where a badminton court is used, there are supports which can be adapted for use for either of the sports. The usual dimensions of the playing surface is 13 × 6 metres, but this can be varied according to circumstances and physical ability. The courts can be marked out in a variety of ways, depending on circumstances, but bearing safety in mind.

The Nytells stress that the minitennis racket should look and be like a normal racket. Suitability of weight and grip apply in just the same way, but the minitennis racket is normally between 5 and 15cm shorter than a full-size racket. One point about this is that the similar standard of quality allows the larger variety of minitennis racket to be continued to be used as the player progresses to the full-size court.

But the aspect of the equipment which has the greatest effect on eradicating many of the difficulties experienced by beginners, especially young ones, is the use of different materials for the balls. These vary but in all cases result in a slower and lower bounce. They enable beginners to make normal full-

powered strokes, within the limits of their own physical ability and development, and without the ball flying away far out of bounds. The beginner also has greater time in which to move to the ball and to execute the stroke which he is endeavouring to produce. These different types of balls vary not only in their consistency but also in size. Some are hardly distinguishable from a normal tennis ball, whereas others are larger, with a diameter of 90mm. The larger ball is generally regarded as being just for the earliest stages. Different coaches have their own preferences for the type of ball to be used, but usually they are used in some form of progression. A good ball recommended to start with in Sweden is the foam-rubber Tretorn Playball.

It was the appointment of schoolteacher Leif Dahlgren by the Swedish Tennis Association to be responsible for the training of instructors that has led to many of the methods and approaches used in Sweden today. That was nearly twenty years ago. He should certainly not be overlooked in any attempt to trace reasons for the Sweden tennis miracle and what has become known as 'tennis the Swedish way'. He recognized not only the advantages of minitennis but also the drawbacks connected with the original very light ball of foam plastic. He co-operated with Tretorn, Sweden's leading tennis ball manufacturers, and they produced a ball which is sufficiently softer but weighs 75 per cent of a normal ball. This Tretorn ST ball

Future Björn Borgs in the making.

is made of a special rubber compound. It is suitable even for training in tennis proper.

Minitennis is not universally accepted as 'the' best early coaching method, and one large club in Stockholm has excluded it from its training programme. But Hasse Olsson, a former captain of the highly successful Swedish Davis Cup team, points out that the majority of the top Swedish players started off by playing in minitennis schools. He also substantiates another of the claims made in support of minitennis, that by attracting so many youngsters to the game at an early age, it provides a good opportunity to spot talent and to cultivate it.

There is no doubt that yet another ingredient, in the search for an explanation for Swedish achievements, is the old adage 'Nothing succeeds like success'. The interest in tennis in Sweden has mushroomed tremendously so that many youngsters aspiring to emulate the results and gain the attendant accolades and financial rewards are themselves keen to attend minitennis schools. Carl-Axel Hageskog, the Davis Cup team coach, has remarked that when Sweden got a superstar in the form of Björn Borg, it meant that tennis became popular and accepted and 'the right talents began to choose tennis instead of the previously popular sports like football and ice-hockey.'

Minitennis is not the secret of the Swedish tennis 'miracle', but it is a good way to help young players. It could well be something to consider developing more in schools, but with qualified instructors. One of the greatest advantages of minitennis is that it enables the improving beginner, at a very early stage, to carry out 'full-blooded' shots. As Hans Nytell says, 'If I get someone who can play a bit on the other side of the net, I can let rip just like a Lendl . . . under these minitennis conditions, at least!'

1 Top Swedish players

There is little doubt that the best-known Swedish tennis player, past and present, is Björn Borg. He is also a very strong contender for consideration as having been the best-ever male tennis player. Borg was certainly the inspiration for the successful Swedish players who have come after him and he initially focused world attention on developments in Swedish tennis. Quite apart from his phenomenal successes at such a young age, he brought his own personal attributes to the game.

First of all, with his long hair held in place by a sweat band, which sometimes advertised a comic paper, and his necklace, Björn was a player who reflected his generation. Björn also showed his individuality in his stroke-play. His two-handed backhand became his hallmark as did the heavy top-spin.

But if traditionalists found it difficult to accept these departures from the norm, there was no lack of admiration for his grim determination and fighting spirit. Spectators came to expect that he would chase every ball to the utmost of his ability and the old adage, that a point is not lost until it is won, took on real meaning.

At a time when some less savoury forms of behaviour on court were being widely publicized through television coverage and often cultivated in other media, Björn made a big contribution towards retaining the previous standards of good sportsmanship and dignity. The excuses of professionalism and the very large sums of prize-money involved, which were sometimes made for unacceptable outbursts by other players, were not needed in his case although they could have applied equally well. In fact his impassive expression and apparent lack of emotion during most vital and nerve-racking moments led to the name of 'Iceborg'. These generally high qualities of behaviour on court have come to be characteristic of top Swedish tennis players.

Björn Borg was born in 1956 in Södertälje, a fair-sized town, some fifteen kilometres south of Stockholm. The young Björn lived there with his parents in working-class conditions similar to hundreds of thousands of other Swedes. He attended the local state school, from the age of seven, like other Swedish children. Also like many other lively young Swedes, he was keen on sports.

As a generalization, Swedes tend to favour individual sporting activities, in preference to team games. There is great involvement in a wide variety of individual physical activities involving snow and ice in the winter. In the summer the waters of the country's 90,000 lakes together with the long coast and archipelagos provide ample sporting opportunities of many kinds. The team games which dominate the Swedish winter season are ice-hockey and a somewhat similar sport called 'bandy'. Bandy can briefly be described as ice-hockey with a ball instead of a flat puck and it is not played on a confined rink but on a larger field.

In his earliest years at school, the young Björn was a keen footballer and enjoyed ice-hockey. But at the age of about nine years, fate took a hand in changing his sporting interests and the future of Swedish tennis. By now the story of how he came by his first tennis racket is well-known. His father had the reputation of being an able table-tennis player and on one occasion his success was rewarded by the prize of a tennis racket. Mr Borg presented this to his young son who proceeded to gain pleasure from banging a tennis ball up against any appropriate nearby near-vertical surface. He had good ball-sense and a quick eye and so, as he felt more control, he attempted to play as often as possible on local courts. Facilities and opportunities were not outstanding, but he persevered and made quick, natural progress.

In these early years Björn had no specific coaching and thus he developed his own, quite unconventional style. In particular, his double-handed backhand was unusual. It came to him quite naturally. From the beginning Björn had fast footwork which enabled him to get to the ball a split second earlier than most and so give him time for his ground-strokes, which rapidly became his great strength. Consequently, a couple of years after his father had given him his first racket, Björn was beginning to win local matches and tournaments. There was positive support from both his parents for his growing enthusiasm, involvement and proficiency. But at the same time Björn was not pressured by them. A few years later Björn was often questioned on this point by interviewers and he repeatedly insisted that this was the case, and that he appreciated the balanced attitude which his parents had managed to maintain.

As his talents grew and became more and more obvious, he became noticed. From the care of his local club leader in Södertälje he passed to Percy Rosberg, who had a great influence on the formative years of Björn's game even before he was a teenager. Unques-tionably as a result of the influence of the American Bill Lufler, Percy had gone on to become a member of the Davis Cup team and then one of Sweden's best coaches. The initial part played by Percy in the development of Björn has not been sufficiently acknowledged outside Sweden. Mention is sometimes made about his having allowed Björn to retain his two-handed backhand, but one seldom hears about his influence on the concentration on footwork to compensate for it. Less still is he associated with the discovery of Stefan Edberg. But all of the world-ranking Swedish male tennis stars have passed through Percy's hands, simply because he has been working with the Davis Cup School for nearly thirty years.

Percy Rosberg started coaching the young Björn at SALK (Stockholm Allmäna Lawntennis Klubb, Stockholm Public Lawn Tennis Club) where he had the opportunity to meet better players and so raise the standard of his game even more. Björn now came under more and more external influences and something happened which had a long-lasting and beneficial effect on his game, albeit very unpleasant at the time. As a youngster Björn was actually banned by his club for a couple of months for the bad language and behaviour which accompanied his extreme keenness to win. This disciplinary action certainly had a salutory effect.

Lennart Bergelin's comment has now become an almost classic quote on the subject of training. He advocates getting the young players 'into the shit', as he calls it, at an early age: they should experience the rough and tumble of a full-time tennis player's life, taking the bad with the good, the travelling, the living out of a suitcase, the many hours of practice and the discipline. Above all, he advocates the value of experience outside Sweden, in various climates, on a variety of surfaces against good players from other countries with their different styles and attitudes.

But already, at the end of the sixties, Björn Borg had made a sufficiently good impression to warrant financial support from the STF (Swedish Tennis Association) to enable him to afford these valuable experiences, which would undoubtedly have been beyond the means of his parents. As a fourteen-year-old, Björn created a record as being the youngest player to win the King's Trophy. This achievement was made all the more remarkable by the fact that in this handicapped tournament he was giving a point a game to his opponent in the final.

Lennart Bergelin was, by then, already endeavouring to put his policy of overseas experience for promising young players into practice. The STF granted permission for a group of young players to tour together for a couple of weeks, playing in successive tournaments in the warmer Mediterranean climes.

It may be argued that this was the beginning of the up-swing of Swedish men's tennis. Björn had an obvious natural ability and devotion to the game. Lennart Bergelin had himself experience of high-ranking play, albeit never quite reaching the real summits. He was a tennis coach of good repute and clearly recognized Björn's potential. They appear to have got on well together as people and respected each other's talents. An additional factor was that Bergelin was strongly involved with the Swedish Davis Cup team. His faith in the prowess of this young player from Södertälje was demonstrated when Björn was included in the team to represent Sweden against New Zealand in 1972. There was, understandably, quite a reaction amongst sports writers at the inclusion of such a very young player, and there could not have been many people who

expected him to win. Up until that time, Björn's only real achievement of note had been that of winning the Orange Bowl, a prestigious championship for up-and-coming juniors, held annually in the US. But Bergelin's decision was well rewarded; Björn played very well and did, in fact, win both of his singles matches in his Davis Cup début.

Thus, at fifteen, Björn faced up to a choice. He loved playing tennis. He was winning more and more matches against better and better players. He had the support of the STF and good coaching. His parents were behind him. Financial prizes in the sport had already become a very glittering attraction. Should he abandon school for a while and see how he got on as a professional player? It seemed fairly reasonable to expect that he could make quite a good living by doing what he enjoyed and was proficient at. Björn decided to give it a try.

At an age when he still had two years remaining in the junior class for tennis tournaments, Björn Borg won the unofficial World Junior Championships on both grass and clay courts.

Björn was ranked in the top one hundred players in 1973. He won the Swedish Indoor Mixed Doubles title, partnered by Margareta Strandberg. Perhaps his greatest achievement in that year was to reach the final in Monte Carlo where he was beaten by no less a player than Ilie Nastase. In 1974 he won the Swedish singles title but in future years he was more concerned with more prestigious titles and that was to be his only year as Swedish champion. In the same year he won in Rome. He was the youngest-ever player when he won the French Championships at the age of seventeen. Consequently, he moved up to the top fifty, and continued to go from strength to strength.

Alongside his many personal victories – he won forty-six international singles titles – there were his many great contributions to Davis Cup matches. These did much to gain recognition for Sweden as a newly-arrived tennis nation, and created a new spirit for his countrymen.

By 1975, the fiftieth anniversary of the Davis Cup, Sweden had participated in twenty-three of them. The Swedes had succeeded in reaching the European final on twelve occasions, and had won half of those, but they had never succeeded in being over-all winners.

In European Zone A Sweden had gained a bye in the first round and was due to meet Poland. There was some doubt about Björn Borg's participation as he had a very important appointment in Dallas. Normally the choice of second singles player would have been from the Johansson brothers, Kjell and Leif, but both were injured, so Birger Andersson filled the gap. As it was considered that Sweden would stand little chance without Björn, he eventually agreed to play, but it was conditional upon him dashing off to keep his appointment, if time ran out.

Birger Andersson played the first singles and lost to Wojciech Fibak in three straight sets to give Poland a 1–0 lead. Björn levelled, only dropping two games in three sets to Hendryk Drymalski. Then followed the doubles, with Björn partnering Ove Bengtsson. The Swedish pair beat Fibak and Jacek Niedzwiedzky in three sets. Björn next met Fibak and dismissed him in three sets as well, albeit 8–6 in the third. Sweden had an unbeatable lead; they were through to meet West Germany in the next round and Björn was able to catch a special plane from Warsaw, to be just in time in Dallas. The final game had no significance as far as the result was concerned, but Birger Andersson increased the final score to 4–1.

The match against Germany was another away fixture for Sweden. It was played in West Berlin. Once again Birger Andersson opened the singles matches and after taking the first set 6–1 against Hans-Jurgen Pohmann, he only won four games in the next three sets. Björn met Karl Meiler and although he won in three sets it was a long and tiring match. The second set was settled in Björn's favour at 14–12 and even the third went to a long set, 8–6. Björn requested that his captain, Lennart Bergelin, rest him from the doubles. Bergelin's decision to pair the far less experienced Rolf Norberg with Ove Bengtsson led to considerable criticism at the time. The Swedish pair lost against Pohmann and Jürgen Fassbender with the rather ignominious looking figures 2–6, 3–6, 1–6. Björn returned to the fray and after losing the first set against Pohmann 3–6, he moved into a higher gear and polished off the next three sets 6–0, 6–0, 6–3. This levelled the score of matches. Birger Andersson was due to meet Karl Meiler. Many seemed to hold the opinion that Birger did not stand a chance. Criticism of Bergelin was revived for 'throwing away the doubles'. Only a miracle could save Sweden now. But, to everyone's amazement, Meiler appeared to be consumed by nerves. Birger took the first set 7–5. He was playing at the very top of his form. He kept his nerve and went from strength to strength. At the time when his very best was required, he produced it. (The expression 'best when it matters' has become a recurring theme in present-day mental training programmes.)

Typically, the harder Meiler tried to hold his game together the more timorous he became. Birger took the second set 6–1. Seeing the match slipping away Meiler fought hard, but Birger held on and kept up his high form. In fact, the third set was more of a battle than the figures show. Birger won 6–2. Sweden had won 3–2 and was through to the next round. Birger

Andersson had become a national hero. He was no longer an unknown. Belonging to that group of players between the end of Janne Lundqvist's era and the coming of Björn Borg, he had been on the point of giving up serious tennis. Suddenly he had played a match which was hailed as 'the most sensational win in Swedish Davis Cup tennis' and which resulted in him being nominated for the Svenska Dagbladet Bragd Prize (Feat of the Year), and within Swedish tennis circles Andersson earned the nickname of 'Bragd' Birger.

The USSR were the next round opponents and the Swedes approached that event with some confidence. The Russians were relative newcomers to the Davis Cup competition, although it was recognized that they had a very good record of home results. Their star player, Alex Metreveli, had lost only four of his forty-five Davis Cup matches, but he was considered to be possibly past his prime. Their number two player was not fit and as the Russians had no depth of tennis talent to choose from, the reserve, Anatolij Volkov, was untried and considered to be comparatively weak.

Once again it was an away fixture for the Swedish team. The event took place in Jormala, just outside Riga, in Latvia. After his previous Davis Cup triumph, Birger Andersson's confidence must have been further boosted by being able to open the Swedish score with a convincing win over Volkov. Björn Borg followed suit by beating Metreveli in three sets. But by now Kakulia had recovered from his sickness and together with Metreveli the Russian pair beat Björn and Ove Bengtsson. The Borg record of achievements in doubles falls far short of his remarkable list of victories in singles in which he only lost three of his forty Davis Cup matches. The Swedes lost 1–6, 4–6, 6–8. Kakulia demonstrated how good a player

he was and, no doubt, the Swedish captain was relieved that Birger had not had to play against him in the singles. Björn soon made amends for the doubles defeat and, after a closer first set, finished off with 6–1, 6–0 against Volkov to give Sweden victory and a place in the European Zone final for the first time in eleven years. Their opponents would be Spain.

Yet again it was the Swedes who travelled overseas; this time to Barcelona. There the highly reputed Manuel Orantes was the star Spanish player. As expected, Birger Andersson lost his opening singles to Orantes and Björn Borg dispatched José Higueras; then the more decisive matches began. Orantes was joined by Juan Gisbert to give the Spaniards an easy win over Borg and Bengtsson. In fact, in fifteen Davis Cup doubles matches Björn lost one more than he won. With Spain now in the lead, Björn faced Orantes. He produced what was called his finest Davis Cup win by beating this very good Spanish player in just seventy-three minutes, 6–4, 6–2, 6–2. Thus everything depended on the final match between Higueras and Birger Andersson. Would Birger's nerve hold out again, as it had done in a similar situation against the Germans? Higueras took the first set, to the delight of the home supporters. Then Birger levelled. Newspaper reports tell of drizzly conditions and refer to some doubtful calls by linesmen; but Birger took the lead in the third set. By this time Higueras seemed to be in poor condition; Birger kept calm and ran away with the final set 6–0. Sweden was through to meet the winners of the American Zone, which was Chile.

At last it was a home match, in Båstad. But there was great political protest about this match being played. Sweden had earned itself the reputation of being 'the conscience of the world' and there was considerable reaction against a team from the land of the military dictator, Pinochet. The majority of Swedes thought that the match should be played and that the oppressed Chileans would gain no benefit from the Swedes giving a walk-over. They argued that it would even give a boost to the regime if Chile appeared in the Davis Cup final. It would be better to go ahead with the match and beat them. The suggested compromise of a neutral venue was rejected by Eve Malmquist, the then Chairman of STF: 'We deserve a home fixture after four consecutive away games. A neutral venue would reduce our chances.'

It was decided to play the match in Båstad. Then came a threat to the life of the Chilean player, Jaime Fillol. The sale of tickets was confined to clubs only and more than a thousand police were on duty in and around the arena. There was an extremely tense atmosphere, quite apart from the tension that would normally have been associated with a Davis Cup interzonal final.

The proceedings opened with Björn Borg playing against Patricio Cornejo. Björn was not 100 per cent fit after an infection. Björn lost the first and it became a long four-setter. The final result was 3–6, 6–4, 7–5, 6–3. In the next match, Birger's opposition to Fillol was rather weak. Fillol seemed to play quite unconcerned about the threat to his life. So, with the score level, the two countries prepared to meet in the doubles. But before it could begin there was a near riot by the protesters and some ugly, threatening scenes. Bags of soot and flour were thrown onto the court. Obviously, this upset the players. Björn and Ove were playing against Fillol and Cornejo, who appeared to be the most disturbed. Cornejo played what was probably his worst-ever game of Davis Cup doubles. The Swedes played well and won in

four sets. Cornejo was still not in good form when he met Birger in the singles and after a 14–12 struggle for the second set, Birger went on to complete his victory in the third; this more than compensated for his weak performance against Fillol, as it gave Sweden an invincible 3–1 lead and the certainty of appearing in the challenge round, the over-all final.

Just who their opponents would be depended on the outcome of the other interzonal final between Czechoslovakia and Australia in Prague. Björn Borg was reported as commenting that against the Czechs he felt that Sweden stood a 60 per cent chance of winning, but against the Australians, only 10 per cent. This remark was not based purely on the relative merits of the Czech and Australian reputations, but it included two other important factors. Firstly, according to the somewhat complicated Davis Cup system of fixtures, if Sweden were to meet Czechoslovakia, it would be a home game, but against the Australians it would be away and on grass. Secondly, such outstanding players as Rod Laver, Ken Rosewall and John Newcombe would not be participating in the match against the Czechs, but they would be playing in the next, most important round.

But for the match against the Czechs, who would be playing their first interzonal final, Australia still had such depth of well-known, talented players that they could field Tony Roche, backed up by John Alexander. Then, by a bitter quirk of fate, both Roche and Alexander were smitten by an infection. Although also unwell, Kodes won his first singles, as expected. Then, after taking a two-set lead, Tony Roche faded into defeat. For the doubles the Czechs wisely fielded a pair which did not include their singles players, who were thus given a chance to rest. The Australians won the doubles, but it was only postponing their eventual defeat, as Kodes relentlessly steam-rollered Roche. The Czechoslovak jubilation over the entry into the final round was echoed by the Swedes.

The final round took place in Stockholm in the Royal courts. It was only the second Davis Cup final to be played indoors.

Björn Borg lost only four games against Hrebec in gaining a 1–0 starting result. The Swedish captain, Birger Folke, decided to concentrate on Ove Bengtsson rather than Birger Andersson. Ove was stronger on indoor surfaces and this was virtually his home court. But although he put up quite a strong fight in a thrilling four-set match, he was eventually defeated. The score level, next came the very important doubles, and the tactics of the captains. The part which the captains play is often overlooked or not understood. As Hrebec had obviously been completely unnerved when being 'slaughtered' by Björn, the Czech captain dare not risk him and put in the huge, cannon-ball server Zednik to partner Kodes against Borg and Bengtsson. This proved to be disastrous and Zednik played even worse than the unhappy Hrebec. He lost his first serve game with three double faults. In fact the score of 6–4, 6–4, 6–4 contained only three breaks against service and in each case it was that of Zednik. One commentator made the rather unkind observation that poor Kodes must have felt as if he were playing against three men.

Björn had then no difficulty in beating Kodes 6–4, 6–2, 6–2 and Sweden had won the Davis Cup.

Without a doubt, as a player in the Davis Cup teams Björn Borg made the greatest contribution to his country's success and growing reputation. In the singles he won match after match and almost all in the minimum of sets and with remarkably few lost games.

Björn's outstanding Davis Cup achievements in singles included a run of thirty-three successive victories. But his great achievements were not only when representing his country. He amassed nearly fifty international singles titles. His greatest successes include six wins in the French Open in Paris, five consecutive wins at Wimbledon, winning both the Italian Open in Rome and GP Masters twice each. Additionally, he won the World Championship Tennis tournament in Dallas.

Björn's total of eleven wins in the four Grand Slam events was only two short of the record held by the remarkable Australian player, Roy Emerson.

However, certain titles eluded him. He made ten attempts to win the much coveted US Open, but he never succeeded, in spite of reaching the final four times. Nor did he win the Australian Open, although he was far less persistent in his attempts in the Antipodes.

It is not surprising that, in common with the majority of tennis players who have triumphed at Wimbledon, Björn Borg regards his first success there, in 1976, as his most important victory.

It is sometimes said that Björn Borg happened to be in the right place at the right time. For the year of his first Wimbledon victory the tournament entries did not include quite a number of top players who, on paper at least, could

Björn Borg the champion at Wimbledon 1976–80.

well have been expected to beat Borg. This reduced entry was due to protest action being taken by many of the professional players. He was also in the right place at the right time to benefit from the growing popularization of the sport through the medium of television. Thus the amazing Swedish result was widely spread to a growing audience of admiring young Swedes, many of whom subsequently sought to try to emulate Borg. As the former champion Sven Davidson has said: 'If, as a youngster, I could see tennis for sixty seconds a year, in a news journal before a feature film, I considered myself lucky. This was in the forties and in a cinema, of course, not at home. But since the Borg era, a television set in every home has enabled young people to see the world's best players in action twenty-five to thirty days a year.'

Björn's Wimbledon successes did not stop at equalling Fred Perry's record of three successive victories. In 1979 he beat the American, Rosco Tanner, to equal Rod Laver's total of four Wimbledon singles titles. Typically for Björn, it was another example of cool nerves winning. In the final set, when he had three game points to level a deficit to 4–4, Tanner caught up again to deuce. Now, although Borg and his coach advocate the importance of chasing every ball, of never giving up, there is no doubt that the outcome of some points is far greater than others. But the psychological value derived from treating every point as a unique one, if really ground into the sub-conscious, is that it reduces panic at crucial stages. Well, there is no doubt that Björn had reached a crucial stage in his match with Tanner. So much depended on the outcome of that game. Björn came through that crisis, as he has done so many other times.

In 1980 he played in what is considered by

many as one of the greatest matches of all time, especially from a Swedish point of view. Once again Björn had reached the men's singles final where he met John McEnroe. At the Stockholm Open, some eighteen months before, the American had destroyed Björn in three straight sets, in front of the Swede's home crowd. But now they were meeting on the Centre Court grass of Wimbledon and with the prospect of the Swedish wonder-player winning an incredible fifth successive victory.

In the first set Björn's play was sub-standard and he only won a single game. The serves and volleys of McEnroe's play dominated, in the style of play with which Björn found it the most difficult to cope. But Björn was nothing if not a fighter and so, grasping every slightest opportunity, he struggled back and levelled the score by taking the second set at 7–5. Now it was the Swede's turn to have mastery of the game and he took a 2–1 lead by winning the third set at 6–3 fairly comfortably. Was the American tiring and without hope in the remainder of their contest? After all, it had come to the stage in this final of Borg only needing to take the fourth set for the championship. Björn reached 5–4 and had two match points in his favour. But McEnroe did not give in easily either. He held, saved the match points against him, equalized the set at 5–5 and the game led to a tie-break. The outcome of the fourth set was held in the balance for no less than thirty-four points. It swung back and forth between Björn holding championship point and John McEnroe having set point to level the score. It was McEnroe who eventually succeeded.

This most thrilling of finals moved into the fifth and ultimate set with the unfortunate Borg having seen chance after chance of victory slip away from him. It happened no fewer than seven times. That was enough to break the spirit and unnerve any great player. But Björn appeared not to be just 'any great player'. His apparent cool control of his nerves, his calm outward appearance and his unruffled resolve to simply collect himself and get on with the job in hand – that of winning – stamped him as a truly remarkable and outstanding player. Even this fifth and final set was a long one, but Björn's determination triumphed eventually at 8–6, with a characteristic cross-court backhand. McEnroe never really seemed to have a chance of breaking service in that deciding set. After a cliff-hanger of a final which lasted for very nearly four hours, the Swedish Wonder had accomplished an unbelievable fifth successive victory in the men's singles at Wimbledon, the unofficial world championship title.

What makes these successes even more remarkable is that they were performed on grass. Whilst there are those who say that the comparatively low bounce on this surface was admirably suited to Borg's style, and this is undoubtedly true, grass was not Björn's favourite type of court by any means. He preferred clay courts and they suited his game better. Taking the French Open title six times, on clay courts, speaks for itself in confirming this.

It was revealed later, by the announcement that Borg was unfit to participate in the next round of the Davis Cup, that he had been in increasing pain during the three rounds prior to the final. Yet in that memorable struggle Björn allowed no sign of suffering to show. Perhaps he worked hard to disguise it and prevent giving his opponent any encouraging hope. It may also account for the unusually poor start which Björn made, before the adrenalin really got flowing to stimulate his muscular activity.

A few months after Wimbledon, in the late autumn, Björn Borg and John McEnroe faced each other as finalists yet again in the Stockholm Open tournament. Once again one of them could, if he won, set a new record of successive wins. But this time it was McEnroe who stood to gain. He had won in 1978 and 1979 and now only Björn prevented a third victory. This indoor tournament had only been contested since 1969 and no Swede had succeeded in delighting his home supporters by winning. The honours had gone to players from a variety of countries. First of all Yugoslavia (Nicola Pilic), then the US for the next five years (Stan Smith twice, Arthur Ashe twice and Tom Gorman), then Europe's turn again with Italy (Adriano Panatta) and in 1976 Britain (Mark Cox). The US took over again with Sandy Mayer making way for John McEnroe's successive wins in 1978 and 1979.

This list of winners shows that the Stockholm Open had attracted top-notch international players. It was now seven years since the seventeen-year-old Borg had made his début. He had reached the final but then lost to Tom Gorman 6–4, 3–6, 7–6. These figures show that both players won sixteen games and that the final set was settled with a game difference of only one. But success at Stockholm still eluded Borg and the Swedes had been denied the jubilation of a Swedish player's victory.

In 1980 it took Björn just two sets to put that situation right. For the first, and what was to be the last time, he won the Stockholm Open singles title.

1980 also saw Björn win the Paris Open and reach the final of the US Open.

Then came Wimbledon 1981. Once again Borg reached the final. But the winning habit stopped there. He was beaten by John McEnroe. Björn had to content himself in 1981 with winning the Paris Open again and reaching the final of the elusive US Open for the fourth and last time.

A year of comparatively limited success followed and only about eighteen months after that Wimbledon final defeat, the twenty-seven-year-old wonder-player from Sweden retired from serious, active participation in the sport.

So ended an epoch.

What were Björn's special qualities? He was strong physically and naturally moved quickly; he had especially strong legs. He had enjoyed a variety of sports as a youngster and was gifted with ball-sense. Then he had the good fortune that his talents and obvious potential were recognized at an early age so that he was guided along the right lines from the start. He had a coach who did not stifle his natural aptitudes nor impose more standardized styles upon him. He was fortunate in having parents who supported him financially at the outset, and in many other ways throughout his career. He lived in a country which had a well-structured system to support and encourage up-and-coming youngsters of promise and willingness to invest money in that potential. He was aided tremendously by being taken under the wing of a coach who had considerable first-hand experience of the kind of future that awaited Björn as he progressed and succeeded; he became almost a substitute father-figure. One might even say that Lennart Bergelin was endeavouring to live out, in his young prodigy, the very highest successes which he himself had not been able quite to achieve. Added to all this was a tremendous determination to succeed, which enabled Björn to overcome the hardships off-court and the struggles in play. He had ice-cold nerves and remarkable self-control. Above all, he had fighting spirit and a will to win.

Undoubtedly, he was one of the best-ever match-players. His stubbornness and coolness in difficulty became legendary. But basically his success depended on fantastic athletic qualities. In spite of an extremely heavy forehand and a brilliant backhand passing shot, he had only a comparatively moderate service and a not very strong volley. But he had the ability to utilize his talents 100 per cent.

For all of these qualities to have been combined in one person was quite remarkable. Björn Borg's personal achievements brought great renown to himself and to Swedish tennis and the effect that he had on the coming years was undoubtedly tremendous. To a very large extent and without meaning any disrespect to the other Swedish players of his time, Björn was responsible for a large proportion of Sweden's success.

The post-Borg era

What hopes were there for the future of Swedish tennis at the time of Björn Borg's retirement? Probably the next best player was Kjell Johansson, but he did not really look like achieving the uppermost ranks. One measure of the success of top players is the number of Grand Prix titles which they achieve. The Grand Prix circuit consists of those tournaments in which ranking points are awarded, the number of points varying from tournament to tournament, as does the prize-money, according to the prestige associated with the event. These Grand Prix meetings are divided into three categories: first the so-called Grand Slam events, Wimbledon, the US Open, the Australian Open and the French Open; second the Super series; and third the Regular series. Both the Stockholm Open and Båstad belong to the Super series, although just a few years ago Båstad was still only categorized as Regular.

It takes an awful lot of searching to find any Swedish name other than Borg's amongst the winners of Grand Prix titles during the seventies. In fact there appears to be only the one, that of Kjell Johansson. Even that was a comparatively low-ranking event in Nigeria in 1978, the year when Björn Borg won three major events: Wimbledon, Paris and Rome. At that time, and during the next few years, Björn was always very near to, if not always actually at, the top of world rankings. No other Swede came within a hundred places of him.

So, for future hopefuls, one had to look among the juniors for possible up-and-coming players. One young member of the Växjö Tennis Club drew attention to himself in 1981, the same year that Björn Borg won his last Grand Prix title in Switzerland. In the boys' singles section of the tournament in Paris, a young Swede celebrated his country's national day and the birthday of his compatriot tennis idol, Björn Borg, by winning the French Open Juniors.

The following year, as Björn was beginning to fade out of the picture, that same young Swede, low on the ranking list and unseeded in the tournament, won the French Open for the first time. At the age of only seventeen years he was the youngest player ever to have taken that title. A new Swedish name had arrived: Mats Wilander. But who could possibly have dreamed, hoped, let alone expected that Mats Wilander would become known worldwide? Who would have believed that within five years there would be serious debates over the relative merits of Björn and Mats, and that many would put forward a case for regarding those of Mats as greater, even before seeing the climax of Wilander's achievements?

In some respects, Wilander 'out-Borged' Björn himself. He cultivated passing shots which could be executed from the most extreme positions of courtcraft pressure in which he found himself. He went on to develop a style which induced a pressure which penetrated opponents' defences, without employing the heavy strokes which can carry with them a heavy toll on the physique of modern-day players. Wilander's reading of the game and intelligent play gave him the edge over more brutal players.

Jonte Sjögren considers Wilander's contribution crucial to Sweden's current success: 'Mats Wilander's victory in the French Open 1982 was the breakthrough for the current generation. Mats's triumph seems to have promoted positive thinking in many people. It helped everybody.'

But even more remarkable still was the fact that it was not Mats Wilander alone who hurried to take over Björn's role at the top of Swedish and world tennis, but that there should be so many others following suit. Within those same five years the Swedish representation in world rankings had changed from two in the top hundred to four in the top nine. Of course, world rankings do not necessarily tell the whole story, and positions can change very rapidly at times.

Mats Wilander shot to fame like a rocket; as well as personal victories, he also made major contributions in the Swedish Davis Cup team. His achievements by the time that he was twenty-one, in 1985, already bore comparison with those of Borg. He had won both the French and Australian Opens, each on two occasions. In addition he had won the US Open. His Grand Prix records showed no less than fifteen title victories, of which three were in Båstad. Nine of those fifteen were in the highly regarded Super series.

In 1986 Mats Wilander won the men's doubles

title at Wimbledon, in partnership with Joakim Nyström. He was also in the singles finals of both the Swedish Open and Stockholm Open championships. The following year saw him win several GP titles and he reached the finals of major events including the French Open, US Open and Masters. But 1988 was his outstanding year. A defeat in the semi-final at Wimbledon was all that robbed him of the complete Grand Slam as he won the French, US and Australian Open tournaments.

Mats reached the number one position in world rankings, although there was always a struggle and interchange of positions amongst the top few players and these included his compatriot Stefan Edberg.

In 1985, Stefan Edberg won his first Grand Slam title, the Australian Open. This meant that there were then two currently playing Swedish players who had achieved victory in such prestigious events. In fact, since the year 1983 when Stefan won all four of the junior Grand Slam events, the victories at senior Grand Slam tournaments have been shared between only seven players. That two of those seven are from Sweden is remarkable.

Up until 1988 Stefan had always been rather in the shadow of Mats Wilander as a senior player. In 1986 he had won the Stockholm Open and reached the last four in the US Open. In 1987 he won the Australian Open for the second time. By getting to the semi-finals at Wimbledon, the US Open and the Masters (a championship held annually, between the twelve

Mats Wilander in 1988, after his third victory at the French Open championships.

highest-ranked players from the Grand Prix tournaments) he was beginning to become recognized as a really top player. He was also winner, or runner-up, in many other events. But he 'put the dot over the ''i'' ', as the Swedes say, when he won the men's singles title at Wimbledon in 1988. Modestly, Stefan has referred to his Wimbledon victory as rather 'the saving grace' of a not over-successful year.

Without a doubt, Stefan Edberg is one of the outstanding serve-and-volley specialists in Sweden and in the world. In spite of improved ground-strokes, especially his backhand, his most effective strength lies in his attacking game. Unlike many other players, particularly perhaps aggressive players, his second service is as much to be respected as his first.

Since winning Wimbledon in 1988, Stefan has more and more taken on the role as the leading Swedish singles player and the one who keeps up his country's challenge among the leading rankings.

Also among the current top Swedish players is Anders Järryd, a brilliant doubles player. At the US Open in 1987, Järryd and Edberg became the first Swedes to win the men's doubles.

There is something of a gap between the international standing of Mats and Stefan as singles players and the third, Kent Carlsson. After the great promise of winning the European Junior Championships in 1983 and then again in 1984, and adding to it the much coveted Orange Bowl in the same year, Kent has never really achieved impressive and prestigious results as a senior. However, he finished the 1986 rankings in thirteenth position, was one higher the following year and achieved his highest placing, sixth, in the Swedish 'Golden Year' of 1988. More recently, he has been retarded by injuries. So that, although Anders

Järryd is a few places below him in Swedish rankings and even further behind in world rankings in singles, Anders is usually much more often regarded as one of the Swedish stars. Also ranked higher, in Sweden, are Jonas Svensson and Mikael Pernfors. Jonas won both his singles matches in his Davis Cup début against the Italians in 1989. Mikael is a surprise packet: he shot to fame, as a virtual unknown, in the French Open in 1986. Amongst the scalps he collected there were Stefan Edberg, Boris Becker and the local favourite Henri Leconte. Only Ivan Lendl prevented him from taking that Grand Slam title in the final. But since, he has not reproduced such impressive results, although he did win the Grand Prix title in Los Angeles in 1988 to become the fifteenth Swedish player to win a GP singles tournament.

But the success story of Swedish tennis in the post-Borg era has not been confined to individual prowess. It is in the great team event, the Davis Cup, that Sweden has aroused admiration, wonderment and maybe a little envy.

Davis Cup successes

After their first Davis Cup win in 1975 there was no rapid repetition of success in that competition. However, after reaching the final in 1983, only to be defeated by Australia, there was great resolve in the Swedish camp. The Swedish team was beginning to show signs of depth.

In 1984 the first round was against Ecuador. It was a home game for the Swedes, played in the industrial town of Norrköping, famous for its match-industry. The South Americans took the lead when Anders Järryd lost the first singles event. Mats levelled the match score. Then came the doubles with Mats and Anders forming a new partnership that was to gain many future successes. When comparisons are made between Wilander and Borg, there is little disagreement over the fact that Mats is the better doubles player. His greater willingness to volley gives him the advantage. With a doubles victory Sweden took the lead. But, because of injury, Järryd could not play his second singles match. His place was taken by the relatively inexperienced Joakim Nyström. Most of Sweden's tennis talent comes from the southern part of the country; Joakim is the only player from the vast area called Norrland to reach the upper ranks of Swedish tennis. He has beaten virtually all of the top-ranking players.

Joakim was very impressive as a junior but never really seemed to come up to expectations. He had very good court sense and ground-strokes, with an excellent backhand cross-court drive, but attack was lacking in his service. Now this young man, close to his twenty-first birthday, had the chance to give Sweden an unassailable lead in the first round. Joakim did not let the opportunity slip and by losing only five games, he won the three sets necessary for the personal win which gave Sweden the right to meet Paraguay next. Mats concluded the victory at 4–1 by winning his singles as well.

The match against Paraguay was also a home match for the Swedes, this time in Båstad. A somewhat strengthened South American team and with Sweden weakened by the absence of an injured Wilander, the new depth of the Swedish team was to be put to the test.

Stefan Edberg, one of the greatest volleyers the game has seen.

Eighteen-year-old Stefan Edberg replaced Mats in the partnership with Anders Järryd, and they lost in this first pairing together. But Anders won both his singles games. The other representative of Sweden in the singles matches was Henrik Sundström, known as Henke. He is physically strong with good ground-strokes, albeit not quite fast enough in moving about the court, so that his best results had been achieved on slower surfaces. Unlike many of his peers, Henke did not launch himself completely into a life of tennis but contrived to continue with his studies alongside the sport. He did well in his two matches in this Davis Cup match against Paraguay, winning them both.

Sweden next had to play against Czechoslovakia. Once again the venue favoured Sweden and the teams met in Båstad. Czechoslovakia's singles players were Ivan Lendl and Tomas Smid. As more or less expected, Mats defeated Smid in a three-set match, but the first two in particular were closely fought.

When Henke Sundström was two sets down and at 0–3 with three game points against him, with Ivan Lendl serving, it seemed that the match was going to run its expected course. Then, beyond belief, Henke gradually improved and hung on, whilst Lendl deteriorated at an even faster rate. As the spectators sensed the change in fortune, the unquestionable value of home-support came into evidence. Incredibly, Sundström ran out the winner.

The very popular Mikael Pernfors, finalist in the French championships in 1986.

In the subsequent doubles, Edberg and Järryd represented Sweden, whilst Smid was partnered by Pavel Slozil. The Swedes went two sets down and the Czechs only needed one more game for victory, but once again the tide of the match turned. The final result was an amazing 5–0 victory for Sweden.

In more distant parts of the world, two of the more classically great tennis nations had been fighting it out for a place in the final where they would now meet Sweden. It transpired that the US triumphed over the Australians and would be the team to travel to Scandinavia. With yet another home-match the Swedes would be playing on a specially laid clay surface court in the Scandinavium Stadium, in Göteborg (Goth-'enburg).

In retrospect it may appear that the Americans did not take this final quite seriously enough. Maybe they underestimated their opponents who were, after all, relative newcomers to the upper echelons of tennis. The US side had singles players of considerable calibre: John McEnroe and Jimmy Connors, backed up by Peter Fleming who, together with McEnroe, formed one of the world's best doubles' partnerships. They had several Wimbledon and US Open victories to their credit. McEnroe had been in great form, with an almost unblemished record in singles matches that season. Unquestionably, the Swedes were not considered to have much chance.

But it was obvious that the Swedes were not to be underrated when Mats Wilander steamrollered Jimmy Connors 6–1 in the first set with Connors winning only three games in each of the following sets. Either Connors's bad behaviour and language on court affected his play or his relatively poor play brought about the former; whichever, Sweden opened the match scoring 1–0.

An even greater surprise was Henke Sundström's victory over the favourite, McEnroe. Not only did the Swede win, but in three straight sets. The turning point came at the end of the opening set. As expected, the American held set point, then unexpectedly lost it; but he soon held another, only to lose that. In all he held and lost four first-set points. Henke eventually took the required two games lead to win at 13–11. The Swede continued to win point after point with brilliant backhands and finished off the match with 6–4, 6–3. What a turn-up for the books! A Swedish lead of 2–0. But against such American opposition, under the captaincy of the renowned Arthur Ashe, it was far too soon for the Swedes to relax. There is a Swedish proverb that, in rough translation, warns not to shout for joy until one has safely jumped over the brook. Now they were faced with the task, initially, of getting over the doubles match, with two singles against top world players remaining.

As Stefan Edberg joined Anders Järryd to face the very strong American pair, what probably concerned Swedish supporters was how the nerves of the young Edberg would stand up to the great occasion of his Davis Cup final début in a match of such great importance to his country. But they need not have feared. Strangely enough it was the much more experienced and accomplished Fleming who gave way to the tension of the match. Stefan dominated the match and was most ably supported by a partner five years his senior. With the exception of the fourth set, the scores were very close. The Swedes only needed four sets to clinch their victory: 7–5, 5–7, 6–2, 7–5. Thus Sweden led 3–0 in matches and had, almost unbelievably, won the Davis Cup for the second time. Sweden had arrived as a tennis nation!

With due respect to the team colleagues of Björn Borg, the earlier Swedish Davis Cup successes had been very largely that of a one-man band. In the 1984 competition there were five players who had all demonstrated their strong abilities and had contributed to the final victorious outcome: Mats Wilander, Anders Järryd, Henrik Sundström, Stefan Edberg and Joakim Nyström.

These impressive Davis Cup achievements have continued. Sweden's appearance in the 1989 Davis Cup final was the seventh in succession.

8 Mental strength

One of the journalists' play-with-words that caught on and has been often repeated, even to the extent of typifying Swedish behaviour on court, was the reference to Björn Borg as 'Ice-borg'. He became well-known for his self-control, especially at a time when this contrasted so sharply with the emotive reactions of such players as Nastase, Connors and McEnroe. Whereas the colourful characters of these players had some entertainment value, especially perhaps among a less tennis-educated TV audience, many people reacted negatively as the behaviour of players became more and more outrageous, with racket throwing, arguing about decisions, swearing, obscene gesticulations and even spitting at the umpire.

Borg never lowered his standard of behaviour on court to such levels; not only did he not act in that manner himself but he appeared to treat it with disdain and refused to become ruffled by it. It is difficult to assess just how much of this aggressive behaviour by some players was due to their individual characters, their highly strung, pent-up emotions, the apparent general acceptance of such behaviour and inability to hold it in check and how much of it was conscious gamesmanship.

Borg's behaviour was not simply good manners. He regarded the loss of self-control and thus of concentration to be self-defeating and wasteful of energy. He also appears to have been well aware of the value of psychological dominance; of being in command of himself, his opponent and the flow of the game. He considered such uncontrolled outbursts as indicating lack of such command and possibly by keeping himself 'above' such behaviour he further emphasized his dominance. Even if his opponents' actions were deliberate gamesmanship, they could also be interpreted as signs of lack of self-confidence and growing concern.

Björn Borg cultivated the ability to be on court almost all day, playing forehand and backhand strokes, in all kinds of weather conditions. This concentration has been described as 'tunnel-vision'. He appeared to be wearing invisible blinkers which shut out all surrounding distractions. Björn has described how this concentration did really need to be cultivated. Already in his teens he was aware of the value of treating training sessions as seriously as actual matches. But it was in these training sessions that he was gradually able to extend the ability to concentrate. The onset of mental exhaustion became further and further delayed. Eventually, this resulted in being able more easily to concentrate during matches, almost as a matter of ingrained habit.

This concentration on 'concentration' was undoubtedly one of Borg's great strengths. He had the ability to concentrate on the point in play: the stroke of the moment. Whatever was going on behind the apparently calm exterior, he seemed to be taking each point on its own equal merit. This mental strength, together with his many other talents and physical condition, resulted in more and more points, games, sets and matches being retrieved from seemingly impossible positions and against all odds.

The value of this mental strength has become more and more recognized in sporting circles, not only in tennis. In fact, Arthur Ashe, the great US tennis star and former captain of their Davis Cup team, has been reported as saying that he regards James Loehr, the sports psychologist, as the most important person in modern-day tennis. It is now estimated that probably more than a quarter of professional tennis players have recourse to a sports psychologist on a regular basis. This figure compares very significantly with that of only a handful of players, as recently as seven or eight years ago. At the same time, there are those who feel that this area of activity has tended to become rather over-exaggerated.

Lars Ryberg is the sports psychologist at Tretorn Tennis Academy. He describes mental training as a compressed form of positive thinking. The aim is to make the player less sensitive to stress and psychological strain. He expresses the basic principle as seeing the player as a psychosomatic unit, i.e. the body and mind together. He points out that the body becomes stiff and tense in reaction to psychological pressure, which results in poor match-play. On the other hand, physical injury or weakness can result in psychological problems, such as anxiety over past injuries.

Ryberg explains that, as all competition involves a certain amount of psychological pressure, mental training is intended to help deal with the nervousness, demands and expectations that occur. But he emphasizes that these phenomena are natural and to a certain degree necessary. It is essential to achieve a balance between demands and performance at peak level. An analogy may well be that of the actor who recognizes that a certain amount of butterflies in the stomach at curtain-up is a necessary ingredient of a good performance, but obviously stage-fright is not.

In the inner conversation which the player conducts with himself, negative thoughts must be ousted. According to Ryberg, it is these negative thoughts which affect body movements adversely. They are confidence destroying.

Lars Ryberg has worked closely with Jonas Svensson. Jonas has tended to have very much 'up and down' results but in 1989 he beat no less a player than Boris Becker in the Australian Open. He was also the player who put Sweden into their seventh successive Davis Cup final when he beat Goran Prpic in his second singles win in the semi-final. The figures 6–7 (3–7), 6–4, 7–6 (9–7), 3–6, 6–3 indicate what a close struggle this five-set match with two tie-breaks was. Jonas showed strong mental control in saving two set points in the third set.

The work of a sports psychologist is to help the player overcome tension and nervousness, whilst building self-confidence. In Swedish tennis there is much talk of 'minus psyche' and 'plus psyche'. The signs of 'minus psyche' are: nervousness and passivity, hesitation, indecision, insecurity, ponderous movement, anxiety, timidity, defensiveness and negative thinking. On the other hand, the behavioural patterns associated with a 'plus psyche' are those of concentration, will-power,

Jonas Svensson, whose great discipline and control enabled him to win again Prpic in the Davis Cup semi-final against Yugoslavia in 1989.

security, harmony, happiness, springy step, self-confidence and positive thinking.

Lars makes the point that it is not only during play that the state of positive thinking is important, but also before and after. Obviously a minus psyche is readily connected with a setback but mental training strives to instil the realization that confident thoughts are needed to avoid the destructive effects of negative thinking.

It is easy to theorize about this, but less easy to put it into practice without help and guidance. Consequently there are relaxation exercises combined with the mental training, in the belief that a relaxed body leads to a relaxed mind. This technique is far from new. It is called autogenic training. It was introduced by a German doctor just after the First World War. It has been revived and popularized very much in Sweden by the Norwegian sports psychologist, Willi Railo.

Lars Ryberg acknowledges that it was Arthur Ashe, the American champion, who first drew these techniques to the attention of Swedish tennis coaches. During the 1975 Wimbledon final between Ashe and Jimmy Connors, it was noticed that Arthur Ashe disappeared from view under his towel at each break between end-changes. Puzzlement gave way to the realization that he was trying to shut out all surrounding distractions in order to concentrate on retaining both his psychological and physical powers throughout the match. For a brief while he was able to practise relaxation as he had learnt to do.

Nowadays, many players are seen to adopt this practice during end-changes. Stefan Edberg, in particular, is often seen or, rather, not to be seen, under a towel by the umpire's chair. During the last decade many of the top Swedish players used autogenic training. This is based on half a dozen suggestions to encourage and achieve harmonious relaxation. The player is advised to close his eyes and to tell himself that his grip hand is heavy and then that it is warm. He should tell himself that his breathing is comfortably controlled and that his heart beat is normal and fine. He convinces himself that the nerves in the pit of his stomach are settled and warm, whilst his forehead is pleasantly cool. The player learns to proceed through these techniques using auto-suggestion to relax the body entirely and produce a state of psychological and physical well-being.

It takes a player about two months to understand and gain confidence in using these techniques. Then the sports psychologist usually continues with a more personalized, tailor-made programme of mental training. Sometimes cassette recordings are used in the training, but care must be taken to avoid dependence on external influences. The whole idea is to be able to conduct an inner monologue.

A somewhat different aspect on which Swedish tennis is currently concentrating is that of ethics. This deals with matters outside what are normally considered to be tennis problems and it deals with far wider and deeper issues. This is all intended to assist in attaining a feeling of harmony, confidence and motivation. Motivation is a word which has been used very often in the tennis press in the late 80s, since Mats Wilander has not produced the same outstanding results of 1988, in which year only the failure to win Wimbledon deprived him of a much-envied Grand Slam.

More and more importance is given to training which develops the 'whole' person in order to induce a feeling of well-being which in turn is considered to be vital to produce successful play. This is called prioritizing humanistic psychology. In this connection it is worth remembering a comment attributed to Björn Borg: the warning 'Don't forget, to a tennis player "love" means nothing' is a reminder of the strains on relationships which travel and absences cause for the professional player. With success there come many other additional pressures.

It is, in the long-run, the brain which controls our actions. However well trained and perfected our body movements and stroke execution may be, they are all in vain if our mental strength forsakes us at the vital moment. After all, it has been calculated that on average only for about one-eighth of the time spent on court in a match is a player actually physically involved in playing for points. But having accepted that fact, what can the individual player do to improve in this respect? Is this mental strength something that one can learn, other than with the help of a sports psychologist?

Probably the greatest need is to be aware of the difference that absolute concentration makes and the benefits that are to be derived from controlling emotional outbursts. But continued concentration is a tiring, wearing process. Much of it has to be developed out of hours of practice. The most difficult aspect is that apparently contradictory process of concentrating on relaxing. An over-concentration on 'concentration' can result in stiffening up mentally and in transference of this sensation to inhibit physical co-ordination.

This inner conversation with one's self can also be used to steer thoughts positively. It is generally agreed, as Lars Ryberg has indicated, that positive thinking will be more likely to produce the results for which we are striving.

However, part of this self-control has to do with emotions and, in turn, with temperament. It is wrong to generalize about national charac-

teristics and there are often exceptions to prove and test the rule. But Swedes do tend to be more introspective than most other races and they do not readily express their emotions outwardly. As a general rule, Swedes prefer to keep themselves to themselves. For it is widely recognized that people living in warmer, sunnier climes tend to be more outgoing than those in colder, less sunny ones. But, as far as tennis ability is concerned, if there is a connection between success and concentration, and if that concentration is partly to do with keeping emotions in check, then the 'Swedish national temperament' is to their advantage.

There have been comments made about Swedish male players along the lines of 'If you've seen one, you've seen them all'. This is coupled to an implication of their play being rather boring for the spectators, albeit successful in gaining winning results. Very often this is intended to apply more to the style of play which consists of very long, baseline rallies. But it has sometimes been linked to the same cool, apparently emotionless attitude on court. There is really no ostentatious personality among the many leading players and hardly any who can really be described as colourful. It may be claimed that Mikael Pernfors is an exception, with his changeable, sometimes 'way-out' hair-styles. But then, Mikael is hardly a typical Swede having spent so many of his formative years in the United States.

Swedes start off with an inborn natural advantage, as far as temperament is concerned, and they seem to be conscious of its value and realize the importance of making use of it. In 1983 study circles were being organized for groups of participants in various sports, with the theme of being at one's best when it matters most. Phrases like 'knowing oneself' were in vogue and mental tension, ner-

vousness and aggression were discussed, along with motivation and joy. Mental block-ages connected with the concern to do well, were analysed, whilst aims and self-confidence were encouraged.

At Gymnastik-och idrottshögskola (College of Sports and Gymnastics) in Stockholm, where the highest qualifications for tennis coaching may be obtained, the curriculum for tennis includes Psychological Analysis. In the outline of the plan for instruction at Tretorn Tennis Academy, in Båstad, mental training is included.

There has been a demand to train further existing tennis coaches in the importance of developing mental strength, rather than using psychologists with only limited knowledge of the actual sport. Sten Heyman was Secretary of the Swedish Tennis Association for many years and he has written about applications of psychology in tennis. Sten tells the story concerning Lennart Bergelin's dilemma, as captain of the 1975 Davis Cup team, in selecting the player for the second singles. He was given the advice, 'Don't bother about which players win against which other players, pick the one with the strongest nerves.'

Sten Heyman emphasizes the importance of self-confidence when training juniors. He stresses also that psychology must be taught in co-operation with tennis experts: 'It can be compared with the installation of light in an indoor court. You call in a lighting expert and you may well get an excellent light that cannot be used for tennis. It has to be set up, not only with the lighting expert but with a tennis man who knows where the lights must be situated, how they should be directed, what has to be avoided, etc. Otherwise the lighting expert is useless. The same thing applies to all teaching by a psychologist.'

Lennart Bergelin played an important role in Björn Borg's success and a considerable part of his input was on the psychological plane. This was the proto-type of the player/coach duo. Bergelin's qualities as a masseur were used to good effect in pre-match preparation, as much for the psychologically relaxing benefits as the physical loosening up. The 'partnership' of Mats Wilander with Jonte Sjögren over several years is a similar example. Stefan Edberg makes no secret of what he feels he owes to his personal coach, Tony Pickard, as far as his improvement and subsequent greater successes are concerned. This help has very largely been in the area of mental attitude. Tony Pickard has no formal training as a coach but he was ranked as number one in Great Britain and played for the Davis Cup team three or four years before Stefan was born. He was also the British Davis Cup captain. He has commented that, of course, players at that level require little training in technique but that his job is largely to keep tabs on the strengths and weaknesses of other players and to keep Stefan in a positive frame of mind.

The temperaments of coach and player, in these examples, seem to have been ideally suited to each other and have succeeded in producing the maximum potential from the actual performer. They have also focused attention on the importance of such relationships in the development of up-and-coming players and the value of the non-physical aspects of the game.

Tony Pickard observing and motivating Stefan Edberg.

As Jeremy Bates has commented: 'Almost all the Swedes who are on the circuit have a full-time coach with them. Mats Wilander and Stefan Edberg have Jonte Sjögren with them a lot of the time, and I know that Jonas Svensson and Christian Bergström travel with Tim Klein, and Stefan Edberg also has Tony Pickard. I should say that 80–90 per cent of the weeks that they spend on the circuit, they are accompanied by a travelling coach. They are not necessarily brilliant tennis players. But, for example, Tim Klein is exceedingly smart, he understands how to play the game and he's obviously responsible for Jonas's success and that of Bergström.'

Other top British players are also aware of this emphasis on travelling coaches and feel that they are placed more and more at a disadvantage when compared to the countries who employ them. They recognize that this costs a lot of money, which may well be coming from sponsors. As Jeremy has said, 'I'm still going to tournaments without any help from a coach, and then I come back to England and there's no one in London to help me with my game. If I come to Queen's Club it can happen that I can't even get a court on which to practise, because members are playing. We don't have a national training centre where we can go and practise. We are so antiquated in Britain. We are so out of touch with what is going on, on the circuit, we do not realize what is required to bring on new, young players. Equipment is changing. It's getting better and better. And now there are dieticians, psychologists and full-time coaches . . . except in the UK. We don't have any of these people.'

Jeremy Bates obviously feels very strongly that this is, at least, one lesson that can be learnt from the Swedish success. He seems convinced that it would be a good investment for the future

of any nation's tennis success in international competition.

It is a sign of the reputation that Swedish coaches enjoy, as well as being a condemnation of facilities available at home, that Jeremy Bates decided to team up with a Swedish coach who has trained Peter Lundgren, his doubles partner, and Joakim Nyström in 1987 and 1988.

Mental training for young players

Just as Sweden is a leading country as far as concentrating on the value and importance of physical training for tennis is concerned, so may they be said to be in the forefront of the appreciation for the need to concentrate on mental strength in their up-and-coming young players. Young Swedish players are encouraged to remember the following points. There is nothing very startling or new and Sweden is far from being alone in encouraging these attitudes. Nevertheless, they may not always be as easy to execute as to express:

1 Chase every ball. Never give up. The 'impossible' return can have a devastating psychological effect on an opponent. You can easily find countless examples of remarkable recoveries; remind yourself of this fact.

2 Make every effort to forget what you judge to have been a wrong decision. Pre-programme your subconscious to accept the logic that by bothering yourself about one irretrievable 'injustice' you could well lose two or three more points soon after, which may be even more vital. Then remind yourself of this fact if you feel irritation mounting.

3 Do not overlook the importance of the pre-match 'knock-up' period. As well as this time providing an opportunity to adjust to a variety

of physical considerations, it is also a most important time to remember all that you know to help to keep in the most advantageous mental condition. Do not worry about some feelings of nervousness. That is a natural part of keying yourself up. Even the most successful actors admit to feeling a touch of stage-fright before the curtain goes up.

4 There are plenty of statistics to support the fact that no player is invincible. Make victory your target before the game and continue with that attitude of mind right from the very outset of play.

5 Try to take the initiative in play and to hold your command over it. If you can manage to get your opponent to begin to fear that you are gaining control of the situation, you are more likely to do just that.

6 Once in the lead, there is often a tendency to be tempted to be cautious, so as not to lose your advantage. This can all too easily lead to being over-cautious, to the extent of altering one's previous style and tactics. Prevent yourself from making such changes and continue with your winning game. However, whatever outside advice is given, ultimately it is up to the individual player to use his or her own common sense. If your taking the lead has caused your opponent markedly to change his game, then you may well have to adapt your own accordingly. The important thing is to maintain your positive, confident mental attitude.

7 Calmly and coolly ignore any attempts by your opponent, or by partisan supporters, to ruffle you; do not allow the smoothness and tranquillity of your mental attitude to be disturbed.

8 Complete concentration on the ball in play at the current moment is the key to success.

It has long been realized, of course, that tennis is not a purely physical game. It has been the combination of brain with limbs that has provided much of the fascination and enjoyment of the game, for very many years. But until fairly recently the part that the brain has played has tended to be associated more with court-craft and tactics. Now, more and more, there is an awareness of the importance of wider psychological aspects of the player's involvement.

The results of an academic analysis of the content and function of Swedish tennis training have stressed that there should not be over-concentration on techniques. They are only one aspect. There should be a greater attention paid to method, psychology and the science of teaching. The Swedish Tennis Association is supporting this by promoting a continuation course called 'Mentally-related Tennis Training'.

There is no doubt that the cool, calm self-control of a procession of successful Swedish players has given food for thought in this connection.

9 Team spirit

Team spirit has long been recognized as an important element of success in team games. The Swedes are convinced that it has been part of their success in Davis Cup competitions. This togetherness in a group, especially amongst the men players, is recognized as being of great importance and it is consciously cultivated as well as coming about quite spontaneously and naturally.

Sweden has also developed another form of team spirit in the team sponsorship system of talented players. There can be little doubt that the creation of Team SIAB contributed both to its members' individual successes and to the Davis Cup team growth in playing strength. In 1981 a large manufacturing company, SIAB, sponsored the idea of the selection of four promising youngsters who would be assigned to the coaching and developing skills of John-Anders Sjögren of GLTK, the leading club in Göteborg. SIAB would sponsor the team for two years. Jonte Sjögren was instructed that if his prodigies could not stand the pressures and intensities of the life then he was to drop them. The four players chosen were Järryd, Nyström, Wilander and Hans Simonsson. The obvious success of this scheme can be seen in the first three players named: they were all members of the 1984 victorious Davis Cup team and have had many personal achievements to their credit.

Team SIAB spent that first winter in Australia, where they played a great deal of tennis and gained a lot of experience on various types of court surface. The renowned Australian coach, Harry Hopman, had gathered a team of players around him some fifteen years earlier, and with great success. To a certain extent, Jonte followed the example of his ideas and approach. However, the hard work in training was less dictatorial than Hopman's is reported to have been. Jonte aimed to develop team spirit and was successful in achieving this through being able to obtain the trust and respect of the young players. Jonte is not too proud to readily acknowledge the not inconsiderable help and advice which he received from that other highly regarded tennis mentor, Lennart Bergelin. Jonte came to be for Mats Wilander, what Lennart had been for Björn Borg, and Bergelin had a vast experience of just how a coach/companion copes with the main task of protecting his protégé from all the daily inconveniences and burdens with which a tennis star is faced.

The idea of the Team SIAB sponsorship was to enable the youngsters to broaden their tennis experience as much as possible; to give them the opportunity to gain international experience, not only in the play itself, by meeting stiff opposition, but in the physical aspects of travelling and living away from

Proud fans and supporters of the Swedish team.

home. The sponsorship also allowed for their trainer to accompany them and to give his support and advice, both on and off the court. This concept of teams has become very popular and quite a few have followed in the wake of Team SIAB. Jonte Sjögren has continued with about ten coaches and almost fifty young players in another team in Göteborg, called the Gothenburg Tennis Talents. More than a dozen of the best coaches in Stockholm combined to develop Team Stockholm and one of the best-known coaches, Tim Klein, is responsible for

Team Ramlösa. There are several others.

Hans Simonsson, the fourth member of Team SIAB, reached the top fifty of world rankings, but did not maintain that high position. Whilst Hans did not achieve really top results, the other three who had been nurtured by Jonte found themselves all together in the top ten world rankings, just a few years after Team SIAB was initiated.

Probably the most positive aspect that contributed to the success of this approach to cultivating top players was the removal of financial

worry in the formative years of these young players. It is not possible to succeed all the time, but often the extra striving because of a financial necessity to succeed has a counter-productive effect. Without those worries, Jonte was able to proceed with the gradual development of promising talent. They certainly repaid the investment of time and money by the high reputation which Sweden gained as the outcome of their multiple subsequent successes.

Time and again Jonte Sjögren has been quoted as saying that there is no magic formula in his training methods. His personality is such that it assists in the creation of a team spirit, near to being in a family atmosphere. The results of his labours and confirmation of his selection of the participants came in the Båstad finals in 1983: both the singles and doubles finals were made up exclusively of Team SIAB members. The team selected to meet Australia in 1981 consisted of the same four young men.

The obvious success of Team SIAB has led to one firm after another undertaking to sponsor a team. In 1988 for example, the Swedish company Parajett gave about £30,000 to assist two promising sixteen-year-olds and a fifteen-year-old in Helsingborg's tennis club. Incidentally, one of them, Johan Alvén, had already won the unofficial world title for his age-group at the age of twelve years.

But in 1981 it was a new concept in Swedish tennis. Nine years later, Mats and Anders are still in the Davis Cup team. Sjögren is convinced that much of the Swedish 'miracle' has been created by team spirit and he regards Mats Wilander as the leading light, who has carried other top Swedish players of his generation along with him.

Jonte believes that together with this sense of comradeship, or team spirit, there has developed a sense of what he describes as 'humility'. It is a word which he uses a lot about the top players. He adds the names of Stefan Edberg, Janne Gunnarsson and Jonas Svensson to the previous team members, when using this description. It is a word which has been adopted quite a lot in Swedish tennis circles.

Swedish tennis stars also take part in other sports as a relaxation from the tension and concentration of tennis tournaments. Indoor bandy matches have become a regular and popular fixture, with representatives of various other sports, including bandy, fielding teams. Mikael Pernfors and Joakim Nyström are regarded as forming the mainstay of the tennis/bandy team, and they are ably supported by Mats Wilander and Stefan Edberg. In November 1987 the team won five matches in a row in a week-long tournament. Anders Järryd and Peter Lundgren (who partners Britain's Jeremy Bates in doubles) were also in that successful team. Their efforts also raised more than £3,000, which went to support Swedish junior tennis. These top Swedish tennis players also often appear together on golf courses around the world.

The togetherness of the group is epitomized by their recent production of a pop record. The Davis Cup team combined with a musical group to sing a song aptly titled, 'Team Spirit'. The team captain and trainer joined with the players in a recording studio in Båstad to form a group of ten tennis personalities to make a record to raise funds for Swedish junior tennis.

Swedish players seem to be more and more adopting the so-called 'Vicht' sign as their unofficial signal of victory. It was Niclas Kroon who introduced this salute. The right fore-arm is raised in front of the face and the wrist is turned to point the fingers towards the forehead, with the palm facing downwards. Kroon used this gesticulation spontaneously, after a victory in Australia. It was a relic of an in-family joke. This was picked up by the press and popularized: so much so, in fact, that Kroon has used the idea commercially and T-shirts are on sale, bearing a portrayal of the 'Vicht' sign. It is now almost at the point of becoming a 'team spirit' salute, a fact which does not necessarily please all observers.

On court there has been and still is, of course, great rivalry between Stefan Edberg and Mats Wilander, especially when they were both struggling for first and second positions in world ranking in 1988. Yet the team spirit prevails. They have even been known to practise together a few hours before meeting each other in a match.

Jeremy Bates, who has played doubles with Swedish partners, has commented on 'the incredible camaraderie' among the Swedes: 'They always train and practise together; they go around together; they are supportive of each other and want their colleagues to win. There is no resentment between them, if one is doing better than another. They are very positive in all they do and they look up to each other. There are so many good players. I've never seen any bitterness or fighting between any of them. I don't know if it's the Swedish nature or mannerism, but they all seem to be on an extremely even keel. They are also liked by a very large majority of all the other players around the world.' Britain's number one does not think that there exists the same spirit amongst the most promising British youngsters.

Danny Marsh, a British professional coach, is also a supporter of the Team SIAB concept. He feels that British players generally seem to isolate themselves, rather than work together. The British need to get into the idea of what he calls 'squads', where players learn to work together and to have an identity other than just self. Danny Marsh has personal experience of being a young member of such a squad at Bisham Abbey. He comments that the squad concept could also act as a protection from too much scrutiny (and expectation?) by the press and others, thus taking some of the pressure off individuals. He stresses that leaders of such squads must be able to motivate, discipline and encourage members to attain high standards.

Danny Marsh also feels that British tennis needs to attract financial sponsorship which will support players before they are able to earn a living from prize-money. Additionally, he feels that there is a need for more sponsorship for the talent spotting of youngsters, perhaps at large clinics held annually at centres throughout the country. Players spotted thus need support and coaching for at least a year to develop their natural talent.

The need for sponsorship even for juniors can be shown by the following examples. The first is that of a young dedicated eleven-year-old in the semi-final of the Kalle Anka (Donald Duck) Tournament. He trains about seven hours a week and for that his parents pay 3,000 kronor (about £300) a year. He is driven the thirty miles return journey to SALK at least five days a week. Additionally there are about twenty competitions a year and the travelling that involves. His equipment is not lavish, though probably not so many eleven-year-olds have three good rackets. He is already getting a little help with dress from his stints as a ball-boy at the Stockholm Open. Apart from the time which his parents devote, they calculate that his tennis costs them about 26,000 kronor a year (about £2,500).

The second example is an extract from a comparison of the typical costs of different sports for young beginners in Sweden. They are based on one training session a week for a year, together with the purchase of the most essential and least expensive equipment:

Coaching	2,000 Kronor	£200 approx.
Racket	200	20
Shoes	200	20
Shorts	70	7
T-shirt	50	5
4 tennis balls	80	8
TOTAL	2,600	£260

PART 2

Techniques
by Mark Cox

10 The ground strokes

This section looks closely at the style and techniques of the most successful Swedish players and analyses them for you to try out in your own game.

Coaches are now more and more realizing that natural, non-traditional styles, grips and strokes may very well produce equally good, if not superior, results. In fact, there is a good case to be made for the fact that the 'miracle' Swedish players and their trainers did not 'follow the book'!

There is a need for flexibility on the part of both player and coach. The new grip, the new swing may seem to be even less effective than the old, making it initially quite difficult to trust in the change-over and to persevere to give the new method a chance. Mats Wilander has told how he lost control of his backhand completely, at the time of his change-over from one-handed to two-handed: his shots flew all over the place. But his perseverance has been well repaid. At the same time the coach must make sufficient allowance for the importance of the player feeling comfortable in his movements and respect the value of 'doing what comes naturally'.

It is traditional in coaching to start with five basics. These are of tremendous importance and it will be a benefit to the beginner if they can be satisfactorily developed at the earliest possible stage and in the following order:

First of all comes *balance* and this is linked to *movement*; then follows the *grip* of the racket. From there we can consider the various *strokes* and finally we can begin to consider *tactics*.

Each stroke passes through the same four stages:

1 The position of readiness

2 The backswing or take-back

3 The hitting point

4 The finishing point or follow-through

Readiness is waiting for your opponent to strike the ball onto your side of the net. Almost all of the time you will be able to face your opponent and be more or less prepared and able to attain the best position. For receiving service you have the opportunity to be completely in control of the situation as far as assuming the readiness position is concerned. At worst, having scurried to retrieve an almost impossible return, you will obviously be less prepared for your opponent's next shot. Between these two extremes of condition of play, it should always be your aim to attain the optimum position of readiness and to have time to produce your shot.

A theory may not always be easy to put into practice, but understanding what is meant by the following coaching advice and always trying to achieve it will stand you in very good stead:

For each kind of stroke there is but one pattern of movement. All you have to do is to move to be in the position to produce just that one pattern. It is just in that little phrase 'all you have to do' that the secret of success lies.

You should practise reproducing these four positions for the different strokes. Try first of all to reproduce them fairly accurately without a ball.

There are some ingredients in every skill that come more naturally to one individual than to another. Some people appear to be born with good 'ball-sense', whereas others are not. Some are instinctively good 'movers' and have a natural sense of balance. If a coach tells a class of beginners that he is going to throw a tennis ball to their side of the court and that he wants them, one at a time, to run and catch the ball in their right hand (or left, if appropriate) *at its highest point after it has bounced just the one time* he will very quickly see which members of the class have ball-sense, good movement and balance. No coach and no book can convert ugly ducklings into graceful swans. There is not a great deal that can be taught to compensate for a more or less complete lack of these basic ingredients. However, there are things to be said about movement and balance which should help players to improve in those aspects of their stroke production.

Grip

Grip is the way the racket is held. There are basically three types of grip for ground-strokes, that is for playing the ball when it has been allowed to bounce the permitted one time. They are the Eastern, the Continental and the Western.

Statistically, the stroke most often used in tennis is the forehand drive. The grip most often used to execute this stroke, by amateurs and professionals alike, is the Eastern forehand grip. It is sometimes called the 'handshake' grip, to make clear how the grip is achieved, although Björn Borg has rather scorned this description on the grounds that there are so many different ways of shaking hands. It has been claimed that the Eastern grip is the most natural and that with it one has more control and so can develop greater power.

All descriptions of stance, grip, etc., are for right-handed players. For convenience 'him' and 'he' are used, but of course the following advice applies equally to both sexes.

Eastern grip

For the Eastern grip, hold the racket quite loosely up at the 'throat' in your left hand so that the face of the racket is vertical, i.e. perpendicular, to the ground. Now stretch out your right hand and wrap your fingers and thumb round the central part of the covered grip area of the racket handle. As your grasp closes around the handle in a 'handshake', the thumb should be somewhere between your middle and index fingers. Thus, the central part of your index finger is on the right-hand side of the handle. Your palm should be parallel to the surface of the racket face. This same grip position can be achieved by placing the palm of the right hand on the strings before sliding it down to grip around the handle. You can check that you have obtained the correct position for the Eastern forehand grip by looking at the V-shape between thumb and index finger; this should be situated on the top lefthand ridge of the grip.

A slight adjustment is usually made by players using the Eastern grip for shots on the backhand, but as that change is so small, the above described grip is most suitable as the grip for the position of readiness. This slight adjustment comes almost naturally and as a

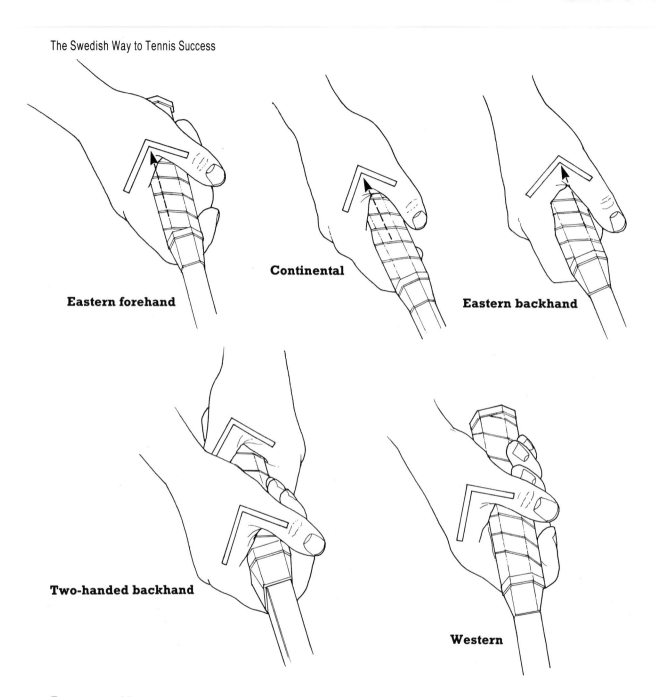

Eastern forehand

Continental

Eastern backhand

Two-handed backhand

Western

An easy guide to determining the correct grip is to locate the 'V' between the thumb and first finger with the appropriate position on the racket handle, as identified above.

matter of common sense. If you use precisely the same Eastern forehand grip as you turn to execute a stroke on the backhand, you will see that your palm tends to tilt to face the ground: that is, it is no longer vertical. With no adjustment of grip this racket angle would loft the ball unduly. To keep the racket face at right-angles to the ground, in a vertical plane, a small rotation of the gripping right hand to the left is required. This results in the central part of the index finger being almost, but not quite, on top of the grip; the rest of the grip position is just the same for the backhand as the forehand. Some coaches advocate using the thumb along the handle to add extra support. The use of the thumb is not really necessary, but if you feel that it comes naturally to do so and you suffer no discomfort, whilst it adds to your confidence, so much the better.

Continental grip

Basically, the grip used for the Continental forehand is mid-way between the Eastern for forehand and backhand, with or without the extended thumb along the handle. Most players seem to find that the strain on the wrist caused by the Continental grip more than offsets any advantage derived from not having to adjust for backhand and forehand. It offers some slight time advantage under pressure, as in the short, sharp volley situation, but generally speaking, the Continental grip is more useful on surfaces which cause the ball to rise somewhat less than average. It is also appropriate for sliced shots – hitting under the ball to produce back spin. One of the most successful present-day exponents of the Continental is Stefan Edberg: he plays the forehand stroke using this grip.

In executing a forehand with the Continental grip, the palm of the hand faces somewhat downwards towards the ground, as opposed to facing towards the net for the Eastern grip.

Western grip

The third forehand grip position, the Western grip, derives its name from the western US, in particular California. The type of surface most common there causes the ball to bounce high. The Western grip is best suited to such a high bounce. Björn Borg's success with the Western grip has popularized its use today.

The Western forehand grip has been dismissed as awkward, clumsy and 'easily exploitable'. But for Björn the Western grip came naturally, and his coaches wisely did not interfere. It suited admirably the stroke which he produced with lots of top spin.

Björn's tennis strokes were affected by his early years of playing table-tennis where there is a tendency to whip the ball. The position of the handle of the racket in the palm of the hand in the Western grip allowed Björn to produce this whipping effect.

In the Western grip the palm faces rather more upward. To hold the racket in the Western grip, lay it on a flat surface and pick it up so that the V formed between finger and thumb closes over the uppermost surface. This results in a grip which is approximately ninety degrees further round to the right, behind the shot, than in the Continental grip.

Hitting the ball

Let us now examine the result of impact between the racket and the ball. The aspects over which you should have control are the angle of the racket face and the direction in which the racket is moving at the time of contact, i.e. at the hitting point. There are other factors over which you have no control. These are the speed at which the ball is approaching you; the angle and what type and degree of spin, if any, has already been applied to the ball, mainly by your opponent's racket, but to a lesser extent by the playing surface and even by the net-cord or, marginally, by the wind.

Considering the two aspects which you can control, we have already seen the effect that the grip has on the angle of the racket face relative to the vertical plane. When the face is perfectly vertical at the moment of contact, i.e. facing directly towards the net, it is *flat*. When the line of direction of such a stroke, at the time of impact, is parallel to the court surface, it imparts no new spin to the ball. As the use of some spin tends to give more control to the shot, a 'flat' shot may well be described as 'less safe'. However, if the ball is struck by a vertical racket face which is moving in an upwards direction, as opposed to being parallel to the court surface, it will impart top spin to the ball. This has the initial effect of creating a forward rotation of the ball as it moves forwards through space, as well as tending to lift its trajectory. To achieve this stroke, it is necessary for the racket to be moving in an upward direction at the time of impact, from a lower swing to a higher follow-through position.

Although the flight path of the ball begins more loftily, carrying it higher over the net, it later tends to dip and almost to hold itself back, thus increasing the likelihood of it remaining within the court-of-play. Then, upon landing, the top spin tends to increase the height and forward-propelling force of the bounce.

When the face of the racket is not flat, but is facing somewhat downwards, it is *closed*. When such a closed face strikes the ball with the lifting, upward line of direction, it increases the amount of top spin imparted. This is the stroke which Björn Borg developed to such perfection and which was the dominating feature of his long rallies. It is ideally suited to extended ground-stroke rallies, as strokes with accentuated top-spin increase the safety margin.

On the other hand, when the racket face is *open* – facing in an upwards direction – it will have the opposite effect on the performance of the ball after it is struck. The spin imparted is in the opposite direction; the ball is rotating backwards as it flies forwards. This type of stroke produces back-spin, or 'slice'. In this case the racket is moving in a forward and downward path, so that it starts from a higher position and continues downwards immediately after impact.

The back-spin, or sliced, shot may be made involuntarily, as a defensive shot, or it may be done intentionally to alter the flow of the rally and introduce variety into offensive play. The back-spin on the ball has the effect of keeping the trajectory low over the net and results in reducing the height of the bounce after landing and it has a tendency to restrict its forward momentum. In fact, a really severe slice can cause the ball to bounce backwards after landing, though this is not a shot to be attempted in normal circumstances.

One more difference about the back-spin stroke is that instead of the wrist being in a straight-line continuation of the fore-arm, it is somewhat bent and raised into what is perhaps most easily described as a cocked position. The wrist should be kept comfortably firm. It needs to be able to cope with the not inconsiderable strain to which it is subjected.

One other change of style which Borg's way of executing the top-spin forehand has introduced is in the position of the feet and body relative to the net. The classic instruction tended to be that one turned sideways to the net, with the line between the right and left shoulders being more or less parallel to the side-lines, whilst the feet were in line with the shoulders, at the time of impact. Björn's forehand top-spin has a much more 'open' characteristic which thus gives more time for striking the ball and returning to the position of readiness which may well be required to shape up for a shot on the backhand. Björn's stroke is made with him almost facing the net in an open stance so it does not involve such a pronounced turn; consequently, the return of the body to face the net is also quicker.

The follow-through

It is probably the follow-through which comes least naturally, even for beginners who seem otherwise to be born tennis-players. It is often the follow-through which has to be developed and even exaggerated. To a certain extent this is understandable as once the ball has been struck it is not so easy to understand the importance of the follow-through. But by continuing the arm movement right through, the likelihood of the general path of the complete stroke being on the right track is increased. The direction of strokes made with a back-spin slice is inwards and across the front of the body, whereas those made with top-spin are just the opposite, as would be expected. They are executed in a direction away from the body and moving outwards. A good follow-through has the additional advantage of the momentum of the arm carrying the body with it and, in turn, the legs, thus assisting in the return to the position of readiness. A very important element of ground-strokes is the transference of the body's weight from the rearmost foot to

the front one, by stepping forward. The concentration on a completed follow-through assists in this transfer.

Borg's 'Swedish style'

Björn Borg was not unique in the use of a two-handed grip or lots of top spin, but they became his hallmark and subsequently there was a period when it came to be regarded as 'the Swedish style'. The use of two hands may be applied to both the forehand and the backhand.

Before he had reached an age with double figures, Björn Borg had been playing ice-hockey and he did not decide to give up that sport in favour of tennis until five years later. This fact, perhaps coupled with that of playing with a racket that was on the heavy side for a young boy, probably explains why Björn found it most natural and easiest to use both hands to hold the racket. To start with he used both hands for shots on the forehand and backhand sides.

Björn's double-handed forehand grip had his right hand near the end of the racket handle in the normal Continental grip, with the left hand fairly close to it and slightly up the handle.

Borg has never been afraid to be unconventional. The execution of Björn's forehand concentrates on imparting a lot of top spin and lifting the ball over the net with a good margin of clearance. Björn always insists that he places a tremendous amount of importance on 'playing safe', of minimizing the risk of error in his strokes. This term should not be confused with 'playing safe' by concentrating one's movements and mental attitude at the time of vital points. The 'playing safe' in stroke production is a habit created by lengthy practice and a conscious policy. He does not aim to drop his drives just inside the opponent's baseline but is content for it to land about a metre beyond the service line. Once again, this is quite contrary to traditional coaching which taught players that they must keep their drives dropping, at most, a metre from inside the baseline, otherwise it was much easier for opponents to attack and reach the net position, from which to dominate the play for that point.

Björn is content for the ball to bounce very close to what used to be described as no man's land, an area to be avoided. But, although the ball lands much further in from the baseline than used to be advised, it has had a considerable amount of top spin applied to it which has the effect of increasing the height of bounce and forward momentum which still tends to pin the opponent back in his non-attacking position behind the baseline. Nor, in any case, would Björn have minded if his opponent did attack the net position as he felt quite confident that, with the accuracy controlled by his style of ground-shots, he stood a very high chance of placing a winning passing shot out of reach of the in-coming player.

After a couple of years using two hands for shots on both sides of his body, Björn relinquished the double-handed grip for his forehand shots but he retained the two-handed backhand. But, apart from now using his left arm as an extra aid to balance, instead of assisting in the stroke produced by the racket, Björn's swing, point of impact and follow-through remained basically the same.

Borg's game was based on one simple principle: the elimination of error. In other words, whenever he played, he went for safety. He preferred to play the simple shot every time. He did not do anything that was ostentatious or of a gambling nature. He was very much a straight-forward, what one may call a 'percentage player', with nothing flamboyant in his play. He played with almost robotic precision and he did not really have a great range of shots. His philosophy was to let his opponent make the mistake. He never believed in hitting for the lines unless it was a matter of desperation. He always liked to play with a large margin for error. This is consistent with his style of play which is based around top spin which causes the ball to pass high over the net, bounding high as well and leaping forward after impact with the court surface. His whole game was geared to safety. His basic technique was consistent and very sound. He was able to make the same shot time and time again, repeating the same stroke.

If Björn Borg had developed his style of tennis in Great Britain he would probably not have been 'allowed' to play in the way that he did. He had what would have been regarded in Britain as an extreme grip on the forehand, the so-called Western (or semi-Western) grip, and on the backhand he used two hands. The value of this, as far as he was concerned, was the amount of top spin which he could produce on both of these shots. In many ways he was the first player to really explore and exploit the value of top spin. It is actually remarkable that he was able to play in the way in which he did, for he developed his style with the old, heavier wooden rackets. One can more readily understand top spin developing more naturally nowadays with the rackets made of modern materials. The changes brought about by more modern racket technology have in fact reinforced rather than initiated the trend set by Björn Borg.

Björn Borg always liked to have his rackets at a very taut tension of about 75 pounds. Racket tension has a considerable effect on the relative resultant speed of the ball after being struck.

For players such as Ken Rosewall in the past and John McEnroe today, who hit the ball very 'purely', almost with minimum effort, it is a matter of 'timing'. But to play the way that Borg played required a tremendous amount of movement, good body positioning and a lot of physical hard work. Considerable effort is required in hitting the ball. Borg was the first really 'physical' player. Consequently, he placed a high priority on physical fitness. He played for long hours, often six hours a day, which he needed to do to develop his technique. To spend six hours a day obviously requires a highly professional attitude. Perhaps he was the first player to be so very dedicated, so disciplined, so focused on what he was trying to achieve. He was probably one of the first real professional tennis players.

The position of readiness

Tennis is a game of anticipation and quick movement in which we have to manipulate a racket in relation to a moving ball. The starting position for shots, the position of readiness, is therefore important.

For this position of readiness, you should have the racket held out in front, pointing in the direction of your opponent, so that you can readily and quickly move the racket to either forehand or backhand, whichever way the ball should come. The feet should be approximately shoulder-width apart, with the weight forwards, slightly on the toes so that you can move as quickly and as efficiently as possible. The ability to move off the mark quickly is a very important element in tennis. It is also important for the player to be relaxed, with his eyes focused on the ball or the opponent, perhaps even both. When a player is in a rallying situation, the ideal position is probably about one metre behind the baseline.

From the position of readiness, take the racket back as early as possible with a smooth swing so that the racket is pointing to the back netting, or wall, behind you. At the same time transfer your weight onto the back foot. Then, as you strike the ball, swing the racket forwards from low to high, placing the weight on the front foot, the left foot. From the point of impact, follow-through in the direction in which you want to hit the ball. It is essential to have a good firm grip and for the point of impact, the hitting

Stefan Edberg stands perfectly poised to receive the ball.

With the weight forward, knees slightly bent, the racket is taken back until the body is sideways to the net. The forward swing is smooth and relaxed through the point of impact, which is a comfortable distance away from the body (see insert) and mid-way between the knee and waist just in front of the left hip. The follow through of the racket is in the direction of the flight of the ball.

point, to be slightly forward of the leading hip, the left hip, and at a comfortable arm's length away from the body. It is also important to maintain balance throughout.

The hitting point is decided very much by three-dimensional considerations. The ball is obviously moving through space and it is very important that a player realizes just where he ideally wants to be, relative to the ball, to execute his next shot.

Generally speaking, for a conventional forehand using the Eastern grip this hitting point would be in front of the front foot, to the side and somewhere between waist and knee height (see illustration).

The net is 0.915 metres (3ft) high at the centre, so if the ball is hit between knee and waist height, the basic mechanics of the ground-shot make it a lifting stroke, even when it is the most simple, as with the Eastern forehand grip.

The dimension of height, in the hitting point, can be adjusted to a certain extent by the use of the knees. They act as 'shock absorbers'. They enable you to raise and lower body height, and therefore the hitting height, so that the stroke can be smooth. They are also 'springs' to enable you to be quick off the mark. During play the knees should always be bent just a little bit. Then flexibility can be maintained for either getting down to the low ball or even stretching and straightening out your legs to deal with the higher ball.

This is, of course, tied in very much with considerations of footwork. It is footwork which enables you to get into the ideal position where you can hit the ball at a comfortable height and at a comfortable distance away from your body: in a position where it allows for easy transfer of body weight 'through the ball'. On impact the racket head must be firmly under control so that the force of the ball, upon reaching the striker, does not forcibly take the racket face out of line.

With the Western grip, where the palm is underneath the handle, it is easier to hit balls which are above waist height. It also tends to make the forehand very aggressive, as was certainly the case with Borg. It is a very strong grip for balls which bounce high and thus admirably suited Björn Borg who played a lot of his early tennis on European clay courts.

But the big difference between this stroke and the conventional forehand stroke is in the stance: the positioning of the body in relation to the ball. This is a very critical area in tennis and one of the most important aspects of the game. With the stroke using the Eastern forehand grip, the weight on impact is well and truly on the leading foot so that the player is sideways to the net. But for the 'Borg' forehand, on impact, the feet are 'open' to the net; he is virtually facing the net. This open stance can be seen in the illustration on page 90.

Most of the basic coaching principles apply to this stroke, especially from the position of readiness, taking the racket back early and swinging from low to high. But in the Borg forehand there is often very much more of a turning of the upper-body and the racket head is dropped quickly in an arced swing so that there is an exaggerated hitting direction of stroke from low to high. Consequently very much more top spin is imparted to the ball.

Stefan Edberg uses the Continental grip for his forehand, which is now relatively unusual. This grip is more commonly used for other shots, like the serve and the volley. In this Stefan is being consistent, because he is a player who relies very heavily on his serve and volley. Thus, unlike Björn Borg, he does not have to be concerned with making major grip changes.

These two diagrams indicate the different hitting positions for open stance on the left and closed stance on the right.

The Continental grip is a similar grip to that for holding a chopper for chopping firewood. Hence the name sometimes given to the Continental grip, to aid easy visualization, is the Chopper Grip. Another way of picturing it is the way in which a knife is held to slice bread.

The same basic principles apply for this forehand stroke executed with the Continental grip. It is necessary to have a good position of readiness, to take the racket back early and to be on balance when executing the shot. The hitting point will be in front of the leading foot but the stance is not so 'open' as the Western (semi-Western) or as 'closed' as the Eastern. It is mid-way between.

Forehand: common faults

A common fault is not watching the ball sufficiently well. It is very important to keep your eyes focused on the ball. Many people say that you should really watch the ball right onto the strings of your racket. Of course, you cannot actually see the ball on the strings of the racket on impact in a stroke, as it is only there for such a small fraction of a second. But it is important that the head is over the ball, on impact; that the head is down so as to assist body-balance. Watching the ball is of crucial importance. Many players, because of their anxiety to see what their opponent is doing on the other side of the net, take their eyes off the ball too quickly. Consequently they do not watch it adequately.

Another fault is not swinging the racket back soon enough and so not having time to swing the racket forwards.

A third fault is an incorrect position in relation to the ball on impact. The player may get too close and consequently have to drop the racket head and lose racket-head control, or he may be too far away and in stretching for the ball be off-balance; he may take the ball too late in which case he is forced to hit up on the ball and often hits it too deep and so out of court. If he is too early on the ball it is likely to finish up in the net.

There are also the errors of taking the ball too high or too low. In both cases this causes the player to have to compromise with the stroke and this generally results in an inefficient shot.

Racket control

A basic drill to help control racket swing is for two players to stand on the service lines on either side of the net and to hit the ball gently backwards and forwards to each other, with the ball bouncing within the service court.

Footwork

One can learn a great deal from studying the footwork of good players. In the case of Björn Borg, he was as light as a feather on the court. For every shot that he played, he took lots and lots of little steps. This contributed very well to the fact that he was nearly always on-balance when he hit the ball, because those small steps allow the minor adjustments which are necessary, since the ball does not always bounce and come through in the way that one anticipates. The ability to make an adjustment at the last split second is crucial. Problems occur very often for players who take large steps as they cannot so readily compensate when something unpredictable happens.

If you do not want to miss the whole action of an exciting game, either as a spectator or watching on television, by concentrating just on the feet of a player, then a video replay may be the solution. This provides the opportunity to concentrate on footwork, or other aspects of the game, at leisure at a later time.

The backhand

The simplest backhand is played with a one-handed grip on the racket. The conventional grip used is the Eastern grip (see page 82). The palm of the hand is on the top of the racket handle, with the knuckles facing towards the intended target. The thumb tends to be along the back of the handle, which gives support to the racket head.

The basics are the same as for the forehand, but the key is in the turning of the shoulders. The player should turn his shoulders round so far that his back is actually facing his opponent before letting his arm come forward naturally, ensuring that the racket head drops to come through to the hitting point. This point of impact should be in line with the right foot, with the player being sideways to the net.

Whilst in the position of readiness, before making the decision whether the coming shot is going to be a forehand or a backhand, it is generally advocated that a forehand grip be adopted. The racket grip should be held gently with the left hand supporting the racket at the throat. The grip can then be changed quickly to forehand or backhand depending on the direction of the ball. In time, this change of grip becomes instinctive, but beginners may well profit from time spent practising the change.

As it becomes clear that the shot is to be on the backhand side, rise onto the balls of the feet, pivoting on the left foot and begin a turn to the side, bringing your right shoulder to face towards the net; at the same time swing the racket back smoothly in preparation for the stroke with arm bent slightly at the elbow. The left hand assists to draw the racket back in a non-jerky manner, so keep it nicely tucked in to the body. The left hand also gives extra support to the racket as the right hand changes to the backhand grip. As the body turns, the weight shifts to the left foot. The back continues to swing until it is facing towards the back netting, or wall (i.e. it is at right-angles to the net).

As the hitting stroke starts, the arm with the racket traces a flat loop to come beneath the ball in a narrow arc. It is mainly the fore-arm, smoothly extended, which performs this shot.

The classic Borg forehand. Watching the ball with perfect concentration he takes the racket back with a high loop, knees bent, enabling him to come from under the ball to impart top spin. The follow through is an extension of the swing finishing above his head. At the point of impact Borg's weight is firmly planted on his back foot.

Bjorn Borg
The heavy topspin
forehand

Just as in the forehand, the transference of body-weight from the back foot in a forwards direction is achieved by stepping forward onto the right foot as contact is made with the ball. The point of impact should be about 30cm (12in) before the ball comes into line with the leading hip. It is at a greater distance from the player than in the execution of the forehand. Tightening the grip on the racket, just before the ball is struck, helps control of the racket head, which should be held above the wrist. The follow-through action of the arm should follow the direction of the intended flight path of the ball. The completion of the stroke should bring the player round to face the net again, in preparation for any necessary ensuing shot. Initially the weight will be on the right foot. The arm comes through in front of the body with the wrist at about shoulder height and the face of the racket is in a vertical position.

Remember that footwork is very important in reaching the correct hitting position and that this is best accomplished by many small steps.

As soon as the player has determined on which side of him the ball is coming, as soon as he has 'read' his opponent's shot, he should immediately begin to turn his shoulder in the appropriate direction: to the left in preparation for a backhand and to the right for a forehand. This early shoulder turn, in preparation for the backswing, is a key to the game.

Common faults are similar to those for the forehand. Most result from failure to get into the correct position in time: from failure to get in line behind the ball.

Tennis is a game of movement, instinct and common sense. So, every beginner can deduce that, in the forehand, if he hits the ball after it has passed his body it will probably go too far to the right. If it is a backhand it will go too far to the left.

Ability to reach the ball is critical. Tennis is about anticipation, speed of reaction, and getting into position fast.

The double-handed backhand

Mats Wilander is probably the best exponent of the double-handed backhand. It is very much developed in the Borg tradition.

Wilander uses an Eastern backhand grip. His main hand is his right hand. Basically, he just rests his left hand above his right hand, along the handle, on the grip. This is a great shot of Wilander's as it is so versatile. He has great variety. He is able to hit a range of shots. Primarily, his main shot is a top-spin stroke. Occasionally, though, he will actually release his left hand and make it a one-handed shot with slice. But he rarely changes his normal preparation which, of course, adds to the element of disguise in the shot.

In the Wilander backhand the left hand is merely placed on the racket to add stability. Other double-handed players, like Jimmy Connors, have a slightly different grip, in the sense that their main hand uses a semi-Western/Western forehand grip. Consequently, with that grip Connors has great difficulty in hitting top spin. Those who have seen Jimmy in action will know that his shots are very low trajectory shots. On the other hand, Wilander is able to come from underneath the ball, thus imparting top spin. He can handle any kind of shot on his backhand. It is the Eastern grip which gives him versatility.

Wilander moves beautifully. The co-ordination of his knees, feet, shoulders and arms produces a tremendous power and consistency. The result is a very fine top-spin backhand. He swings forward at the ball on a low-to-high, inside-to-outwards direction. He has

From the position of readiness the racket is taken back with the left hand supporting the racket at its throat until the shoulders are fully turned. Step forward on to the right foot as the ball is struck, the hitting point slightly in front of the leading hip. The follow through finishes high, lifting the ball over the net.

Mats Wilander's backhand, one of the game's best strokes, is played with two hands: an eastern grip with the right hand and the left hand merely placed on the racket to add stability. It is a perfectly co-ordinated stroke, commencing with the knee bend and shoulder turn, the racket moving through the ball from low to high, his left hand coming off the handle after impact.

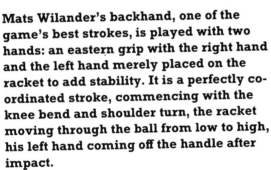

perfect concentration with his eyes being riveted to the ball. It is salutory to look at a picture which shows the head of a great player in action. You will notice that the head invariably stays stationary until after impact, as does Mats Wilander's.

As the ball comes to him, he takes the racket back, turning his shoulders and also taking the weight onto his back foot. Then, as he moves to strike the ball, he brings the racket head forward, pushing off on his back foot and taking the weight onto his front foot. At impact, the face of his racket is perpendicular to the court surface. This is an important point! It is the same with Borg: the hitting point of the racket face onto the ball is perpendicular. Obviously, the trajectory of the stroke is from low to high. The racket head then lifts up behind the ball, the racket face turns over in fact. The stroke has a very high line of direction so that Mats finishes up with the racket way up above his head, in front of his face, although not covering his eyes.

It is interesting evidence of the fact that Wilander only uses the left hand for stability that after impact the left hand comes off the racket grip. Björn Borg does exactly the same thing, the left hand leaving the grip to allow a full follow-through. It is the full extension of the racket arm behind the ball that is important.

There is great similarity between the backhand strokes of Borg and Wilander, although Wilander has greater variety than Borg. Wilander can adjust the degree of top spin more effectively by increasing the sweep of his back-swing. Alternatively, he can reduce the back-swing if he is rushed. Mats now has a tendency to take more balls on the rise, particularly on hard courts.

The characteristics of Wilander's backhand are consistency and effectiveness. It is a very confident shot and he can cope with almost any type of shot to his backhand, whether it be a return of service or ground-stroke in a rally, and return it with added velocity. Wilander's backhand is an improvement on a shot originated by Borg.

Stefan Edberg's backhand is single-handed, although at one time he did use two hands. Like Björn Borg, he was coached by Percy Rosberg. But when he was fourteen he changed to a single-handed backhand, and now has one of the best single-handed backhands in the game. So, in a sense, that is a further evolution of the backhand.

In recent years, Mats Wilander has developed his sliced backhand most effectively. The mechanics of this shot involve hitting the ball from above, down the back of the ball, ending up lower. So, the line of direction of the stroke is totally different. This difference in the movement of the racket head is shown in the illustration on page 124. In this stroke the shoulders stay sideways, at all times, following the flight of the ball: i.e. the shoulders staying in line with the flight of the ball. The follow-through is not so long, the body weight is on the front foot, the right foot.

There are advantages and disadvantages to the two-handed backhand.

Having two hands on the racket gives more strength and stability. Therefore it should be

As the ball approaches, take the racket back with its face open, turning the shoulders until they are sideways to the net. The trajectory of the swing is forward and downward through the point of contact. The shoulders remain sideways to the net throughout the stroke, the racket head following the flight of the ball.

Mats Wilander, with total concentration, his eyes glued to the ball, is leaning into a sliced backhand.

possible to execute the shot more successfully, particularly in returning very hard shots such as a fast service, a smash or a powerful ground-shot. Having two hands on the grip should result in better racket-head control and allow the player to execute a better shot in response. It is also an important point, in the context of the modern game, that using two hands allows the player to impart far more top spin, with power. This is perhaps the main theme that has been introduced by Borg and Wilander. They are able to play a game which has not only top spin, but also power. The two hands on the racket help to develop an explosiveness, a speed of shot.

Having two hands on the racket also enables the player more easily to conceal the length, direction and type of shot being played. That applies not only to the basic ground-shots, in terms of direction and amount of spin, but also, in Wilander's case, to the lob and the drop-shot. Wilander is also adept at producing a sliced block-shot. All of these shots can be played with a great deal of disguise, having two hands on the racket.

The disadvantages are that one does not have quite the same amount of reach and one is more vulnerable to a sliced service, or some other shot from one's opponent which produces a similar effect. Borg had great difficulty in dealing with McEnroe's sliced service. He was certainly limited on his backhand side, not being able to get to the ball so well. Borg made up for it with superb footwork, anticipation and instinctive reaction, but in the latter days he had great difficulty with McEnroe, simply because of the wide ball that came to his back-hand side. Also, with two hands on the racket, a short ball, a low shot, is more difficult to play, since it is difficult to stretch forward and maintain racket-head control.

For a player who uses two hands on the back-hand and does not have the ability to make the stroke confidently with one hand, then sliced shots are difficult to make. It is not a natural shot to play with two hands; the left hand has to leave the racket to execute a sliced shot, as Wilander learnt. Also it becomes difficult when volleying to get the correct body position and to hold the racket face in the correct position behind the ball. It also makes it less easy to manipulate the racket in close-up net-play when quick reactions are necessary for good volleying.

Some common faults

In ground-strokes common faults include:
   dropping the racket head
   getting too close to the ball
   poor grip
   not getting sideways to the ball (i.e. tending to be too 'flat on')
   hitting the ball too late
   letting the ball drop too much resulting in dropping the racket head
   poor wrist control
   not bending the knees

The service

The serve is the most important stroke of all, simply because it is the shot which puts the ball in play. It is the start of each rally and if you never lose your serve game you cannot lose the set until the tie-break, where the same applies. If you win your service points, you cannot lose the tie-break.

From the tactical point of view also, it is vital that a player is able to master the power, direction and control of the serve. For, in the case of this shot, he knows, or should know, where the ball is going. At the same time, the receiver is not sure. He might have an inclination as to where the ball is going but he is not one hundred per cent certain. That element of uncertainty is a very important part in the value of the service.

How you stand to serve is very similar to how you would stand to throw a ball. There is great similarity between the service action and that of throwing a ball over-arm: not a cricket bowling action, but an over-arm throw. To do this, one most naturally assumes a sideways stance, with the feet approximately shoulder-width apart.

For an indication of the direction in which a properly executed serve is likely to take, imagine a line being extended from the toe of the back foot through the toe of the front foot and on towards the opposite end of the court. By thus arranging the relative position of the feet we should be correctly placed in order to serve the ball in the intended direction.

The position of the feet when taking up position to serve, just behind the base line, in singles play is most usually very close to the middle point of the base line in order to be centrally placed to deal with the opponent's return. In doubles, however, the serving position will probably vary from that central mark as the serving partner should be able to cover part of the court. The toe of the front foot should be close to the line, just leaving sufficient space as a margin to avoid foot-faulting.

Practice should always be done properly; do not allow sloppy habits to creep in. When practising your serve, make sure that you keep behind the service line and on the correct side of the centre mark. The serve is a shot that you can practise on your own. It is the shot which has the most intimidating effect on beginners and yet it is possibly the one which shows the greatest improvement with practice.

The grip to use is the Continental grip, or 'chopper' grip (see page 82). The fingers should be slightly more closed on the racket grip to allow more flexibility of the wrist – a snap action – 'throwing' the racket-head at the ball.

Three types of serve

100

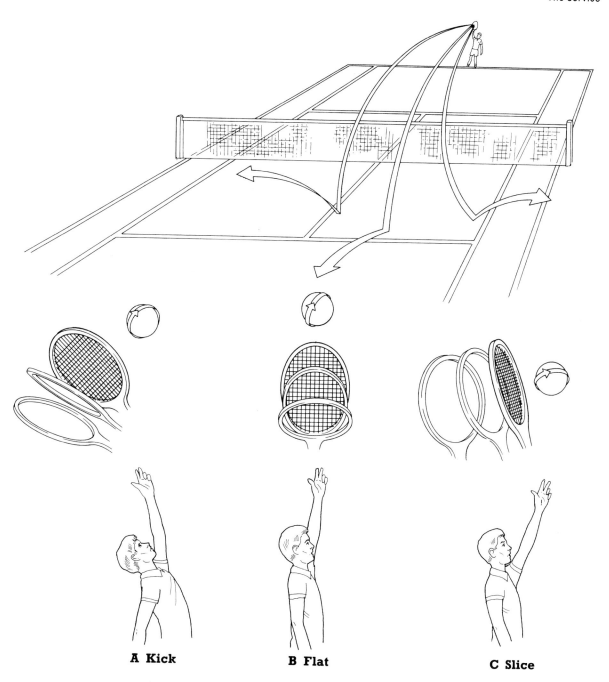

A Kick

B Flat

C Slice

The serve sequence
  The racquet swing should be relaxed and rhythmical throughout, accelerating from the 'back-scratching' position. The ball rests lightly in the fingertips, as shown above.

The swing

The normal sequence of the stroke is for the racket head to drop, like a pendulum in an arc, so that the elbow can be bent enabling the racket to drop behind the back of the server. This is commonly called the 'back-scratching position' by coaches trying to describe the placing of the racket, as in that position one could actually do just that. From there the racket head is 'thrown' upwards at the ball, with a transference of weight from the back foot, pushing up on the front foot. The follow-through for the right-handed server is down the left-hand side of the body.

The hitting position

The hitting position is achieved in combination with the 'ball toss'. The left hand, the one not gripping the racket, holds the ball and places it in the air with a lever movement of the arm. The ball should be tossed only as high as is necessary for the serve to be hit just slightly

below the maximum height of that toss – just as it begins to drop. The position of the hitting point in relation to the body is slightly to the side and slightly to the front, in the sideways position, so that if the ball were allowed to bounce it would fall inside the court to the right of the body. The ball toss needs to be forwards of the body so that the whole body-weight moves forwards into the ball as the serve is executed. The practice of the server following the service action by almost falling forwards and continuing to the net was once very much a feature of the 'serve and volley' type of game, but this is not now quite so prevalent since the influence of Borg and the greater concentration on longer rallies involving long exchanges from the back of the court. However, the forward movement into the ball is still very much an integral part of the service action.

Common faults

The problems that many, if not most, players tend to have with the serve can be traced to:

1 Grip: many beginners assume a forehand grip which does not allow them to 'throw' the racket head at the ball. It also causes the hitting point to be lower than the fully extended arm.

2 Poor throwing-action: in other words, the racket does not arc down behind the back, often resulting in more of a 'cricket bowling'

Edberg starts his serve with an extreme
sideways stance. He first takes his weight
on to his back foot and, as he puts the ball
into the air, he arches his back transferring
his weight forward. He throws his racket
from the back-scratching position,
reaching to hit the ball at maximum height.
The follow through launches him into the
court on his way to the net.

action. In extreme cases the serve is only a 'push' shot, up in front of the face, with virtually no swing at all.

3 Ball-toss: many players have difficulty in putting the ball into the right place – it can be too high, too low, too far left, too far right, too far forwards or too far back over the head. The toss-up action appears to be very simple, but to regularly and reliably place the ball just where you want it requires a mixture of good co-ordination and lots and lots of practice. Control of the toss-up is very important: this innocent-looking little ingredient in the most vital shot should not be underestimated. At the same time it is the easiest part of the game to practise. You do not need to be on a tennis court and you do not really need a racket, although if you follow the advice of always practising 'properly', holding the racket in the other hand completes the physical composition and feel of the situation.

If the toss does not put the ball in the right position, there has to be a compromise in the swing. The ball should be held lightly: in fact, hardly held at all, just resting in the palm. The wrist does not participate but remains inactive. The upward swing of the tossing arm alone provides propulsion to the ball. The fingers and wrist of the hand holding the ball are in a state of neutrality during the toss. The secret of the ball-toss is to be able to put the ball in the same relative position every time.

It is important for the arm to be fully extended at the time of impact. The ball should be struck at maximum height, without over-stretching.

If you do not like your toss-up of the ball, simply let it fall to the ground without completing your service stroke and try again. With practice you will soon find that this becomes less and less necessary.

Borg has compared his service action with that of throwing a javelin. He has also rightly stressed that rhythm and relaxation are essential ingredients of a good service: it is important on the serve to allow both arms, the arm with the racket and the hand holding the ball, to move in a synchronized, relaxed way. In Borg's service the full shoulder-turn is an important part of his stroke. This turn occurs as the player is using the throwing action with the racket head. The player should be hitting upwards on the ball; it is an upwards movement when 'throwing' the racket head, not a downwards throw. This is a very important point to understand and strive to effect.

It is most important that the service is a continuous, fluent flowing action. One of the hardest things about the serve is to co-ordinate the racket and the ball-toss. One can be coached how to stand and how to swing and follow-through until a beautifully 'correct' action results; advice and lots of practice can control the ball-toss to a satisfactory standard of reliability; but crucial to success is feeding the ball-toss into the desired flowing swing, to strike the ball at just the right hitting point, in a continuous, rhythmic swing.

For most beginners, even so-called 'natural' players and those with the gift of ball-sense, this co-ordination requires lots of practice. Practise tossing up the ball in any convenient place; practise also without a ball, to achieve a flowing swing which incorporates the back-scratcher. Then put the two ingredients together and persevere. Even when you have succeeded in wedding those two actions into a service which more or less regularly places the ball over the net in the desired direction of the appropriate service box, there is still a lot of practice to be done. The easiest is that of placing targets fairly close to the service line, in the corners; one near the centre line and another near the inner tram line. You could add a third, midway between them.

To a large extent, the position where the ball is placed by the upward toss will dictate the type of serve which the player utilizes.

There are basically three types of serve:

1 The flat serve: examined and described above

2 The sliced serve: where the racket face is coming round the side of the ball

3 The top-spin serve: where the racket face is moving across the ball and up on the ball. If we imagine that we are looking at the ball as being represented by the face of a clock, the racket face is moving from eight o'clock across to two o'clock.

For the sliced serve the ball-toss must be further to the right to allow the racket to come round to the side. For the top-spin serve (or kick serve) the ball must be tossed up rather more over the head of the server so that he has to arch his back, allowing the racket face to come more easily from underneath the ball, i.e. from eight o'clock to two o'clock to provide the spin.

The value of these different serves and their resultant effects depends on the various court surfaces and their current condition. A sliced serve is invariably useful on a court surface which is quite quick, like a grass court, where the ball moves away very quickly as the spin takes effect. The greater the slicing action the greater the movement of the ball through the air, resulting in the ball moving away quickly to the left. On the other hand, in the case of the kick serve, because it has top spin, the ball will pass high over the net and when it bounces it will break to the right, kicking high. Its par-

ticular value lies in its usefulness as a controlled second serve.

It is often said that a player is only as good as his second serve. For a secure, safe and effective second serve allows a player to play the first serve with very much more confidence. Indeed, at the press conference after Mats Wilander had played in the 1989 Davis Cup semi-final against Yugoslavia, one of the journalists who knew that Mats had his birthday in a few days time asked him what he would like as his ideal gift; after a momentary pause and with a wry grin, Mats replied, 'Do you know where I can get a good second serve?' But when statistics show that in the 1988 Paris Open final, for example, Wilander served into court the incredibly high figure of 97 per cent of his *first* services, then perhaps his need is not too great.

Stefan Edberg is reckoned to have the best second serve in the game. His kick second serve is aggressive, consistent and loaded with spin. In the photographs on pages 104 and 105 notice the way in which he stands sideways, the way in which he shifts his weight and the way in which he arches his back.

The arching of the back allows Edberg to hit upwards on the ball. As he hits upwards, he pushes up on his front leg and lifts himself off the ground. The arm makes a very strong upward brushing motion. Even though hitting a second serve, the energy that is put into it, the strength of the upward motion, is equally as strong as the first serve. The difference is that the second serve has a greater amount of spin imparted to it to add control.

The illustrations show that Edberg's arm is fully extended. It almost forms a straight-line with his left leg. This is an indication of a fundamentally solid, well-timed service motion.

At the time of impact, Edberg's shoulders

are still at an angle to the net, in other words, sideways on. One of the problems encountered in many players is that they are too 'flat on' when they hit the ball; they 'open' their shoulders to face the net too soon. As a result, what happens is that they rely too much on the hitting arm to generate pace and spin, instead of using their entire body.

As a general rule, aim to place your serve as deeply as possible into the service box, allowing yourself a sufficient margin of error to match your control. Your main aim should be to put your opponent on the defensive or, failing that, to prevent him from immediately being able to attack you.

Normally it is best to direct your serve to the corners of the service box; but use variety, which could include deliveries into the central part of the service line of the box. By this variation your opponent is kept guessing and must retain a more or less central position for his return of service, thus allowing you to angle your serve out to the side lines to drive him away from the centre of his court and so open it up for your second shot. Then, if he edges outwards to cover that eventuality, you can attack down the middle line. Remember the importance of the service lies in the fact that you hold the initiative and have the first chance to dominate the outcome of the point which you put into play. Similarly, having the chance to position the opening shot gives you an opportunity, straight away, to use any existing crosswind to accentuate the natural drift away, which is associated with a sliced serve.

Take note of any particular weakness your opponent may have on his forehand or backhand. Take into consideration the left- or right-handedness of your opponent when he serves as this will influence his choice of direction of attack.

Some Common Faults

In the serve common faults include:
  'round arm' action
  gripping the racket as though holding a frying pan, which does not allow full extension of the racket arm
  hitting the ball at too low a point
  feet too close together, so that the body cannot get fully into the stroke
  feet too far apart so that they become immovable and weight transference is difficult

12 Return of service and the volley

Return of service

This stroke is probably neglected in practice even more than is the service. Yet in many ways it is equally important.

The return is different from other strokes in many respects. In theory, of course, it resembles the ground-strokes, but it is a stroke which often has to be played very quickly. The reaction has to be fast. The ability to react to the service is vital, so that the readiness position is important.

The grip for the return of service depends a lot on the style of play of the player. Most players stand prepared for a forehand or backhand. Lefthanders often stand with a backhand grip because that is what most of the serves seem to come to. Choose the one that you feel is more often going to be needed, holding the racket handle loose.

Normally, stand just behind the baseline to receive a first service. The strength of your opponent's service and the bounce will determine how far behind the baseline you should stand. For the second serve, which is normally somewhat slower, you can probably stand a little bit further forward, sometimes inside the baseline. Obviously, the harder the serve then the shorter the time for reaction becomes and in consequence the take-back swing also becomes shorter.

Where to stand for the return of serve will also be affected by the type of shot you would ideally like to play. If you want to make a top-spin return of serve, if this is your normal shot, then you are going to require more time and will need to stand further back than someone who usually uses a chop, or sliced return, which is executed with a considerably shorter backswing. The racket head travels a shorter distance, producing almost a block-shot. If you are going to play a backhand top-spin return, then you will need even more time.

As time is of the essence in the stroke for the return of service, there is not much time for footwork. This needs to be very short and snappy, normally involving one or two sideways steps. A general rule to remember in positioning for the return of service, and other strokes as well, is that it is easier if you have to move forward to adjust your position for execution of the stroke than to have to retreat.

The secret for the return of service is to get the shoulders round, with the upper body turning, even though one does not actually have time to get the feet into the ideal position. The turning of the upper body is critical. A great exponent of this is the American champion, John McEnroe. Another is Mats Wilander, particularly on the backhand side.

One of the keys to a good return of service is racket-head control. Mats Wilander, using two hands, supports the racket head with his left hand. A firm wrist is important in the striking hand. The point of impact, as with the ground-strokes, is in front of the body, so that the body-weight is coming forward. This actually allows a shorter swing. With the body-

Anders Järryd, a fine returner of the serve, shows extreme alertness when ready to receive the ball. As he has little time to prepare, the swing is abbreviated. He blocks the ball with a firm grip and footwork is reduced. It is the upper body rotation which effects the shot.

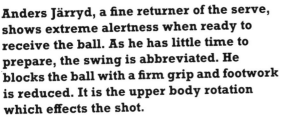

weight coming forward it is possible to achieve the desired results, with a firm impact which directs the ball back to the part of the court that you select for your return of service.

If your opponent is advancing to the net, coming in behind his serve, then the trajectory of the return should be much lower with the aim to get the ball to bounce shorter, near the service line, at the feet of the in-coming server.

On the other hand, if the server is staying back behind the baseline, then it is important to create as much depth as possible in returning the service. Thus the server is far less able to attack and advance to a possibly dominating net position.

If your opponent's delivery is very fast, your reaction time will consequently be shorter, necessitating even greater concentration on the ball so that you can move as quickly and instinctively as possible towards where the ball is likely to land. It is important to be focusing your eyes on the ball as it is struck.

This stroke is critical in doubles play. With Anders Järryd being one of the very top-ranking doubles players, having now won every Grand Slam doubles title, it is not surprising that the return of service is a strong weapon in Anders's repertoire. The illustrations show Järryd's return of service and are well worth studying carefully.

The approach shot

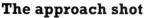

The approach shot is a transitional shot. It is a shot which assists the player to move from the back court to the forecourt, towards the net position. It is obviously a good shot for the advancing player, for the better player. It is also invaluable to the aggressive type of player, who performs well in the net position.

Quite simply, an approach shot is any shot that you make in the back or mid-court area in order to approach the net. It can be made on the forehand or the backhand. It is normally tackled more aggressively on the forehand, either flat or with top spin, whereas on the backhand the approach is more often made with a sliced or blocked shot. This backhand resembles more a blocked return of serve. It has a more abbreviated backswing and the ball is hit out in front with a shorter follow-through. It is very important to place the approach shot near your opponent's baseline, otherwise he can use an aggressive shot in reply. As a generalization, the closer to the tram-line, or side-line, the ball is placed, the better.

To sum up the approach shot: placing is absolutely critical; the back-swing, especially on the backhand tends to be shorter to produce more of a block-shot, with a little bit of under-spin slice or back spin. On the forehand side, because it is easier to rotate the body into the ball, the shot tends to be far more aggressive and uses far more top spin. Essentially the stroke is the same as for other ground-strokes, but it is important to meet the ball in front of the body to allow a continuous movement in towards the net.

The volley

The volley is made before the ball has bounced on your side of the net. There is often far less time to prepare for the stroke and the racket head may be subjected to greater force from your opponent's shot.

The usual grip for the volley is the Continental. Some players use a grip that is more to the backhand side of the Continental, which allows them to open their racket face more on the forehand volley, especially for the low one.

The reason for using the Continental grip is that, as this shot is played closer to the net, you are very much nearer to your opponent; there is less time to think, so that it becomes a much more instinctive shot and there is much less time in which to change the grip on the racket. The Continental grip is a good composite grip which allows you to play both forehand and backhand without a change.

In the position of readiness for the volley, the knees are slightly more flexed and somewhat wider apart than for ground-strokes. The player has to be ready to spring, like a cat, most probably in a forwards direction. It is a help in the backhand volley if the left hand cradles the racket around the throat as the racket is taken back and the shoulders turn. But, essentially, just as with the forehand volley, the take back is a very short action.

It is helpful with the volley to imagine that you are simply going to catch the ball in your hand, in front of the net. The volley is often played close to the net and in this position there would be very little movement of the hand in trying to catch the ball. The same applies with the racket face which meets the ball more or less flat on (see page 114). A firm grip is needed on the racket. The hitting point is well in front of the body. The key, with the volley, is that the racket face should be parallel with the net at

Stefan Edberg is one of the finest volleyers in the world, especially on the backhand as depicted here. As the ball approaches, he turns his shoulders and, with very little swing of the racket, steps aggressively forward to meet the ball well out in front of the body. The ball is hit with firm racket head control.

the point of impact, particularly with the low volley. The higher the ball, the more the racket head can be held above the wrist. Ideally, the racket head should always be above the wrist when executing the volley, however low the point of impact for the shot may have to be. This necessitates bending the knees in order to get down to the shot. There is an obvious advantage in striking the volley from above the height of the net, so that quick movement to a position in which this is possible is very important.

The lower the ball comes over the net, the more one has to bend one's knees and 'open' the racket face, imparting just a little bit of bottom spin, or slice; this gives more control over the ball and the aim is to get the ball back as deeply as possible. By achieving this, one is keeping the opponent 'honest', to use a tennis term.

The basic elements of the volley are: the take-

back swing is very short; the upper body is turned to the right, for the forehand, with the elbow slightly bent but relaxed; the racket head is raised and slightly opened; the racket then moves forwards into a type of blocking shot. At the point of contact, the elbow is relatively straight, out in front of the body, with the wrist held very firmly. The racket head itself is more or less vertical, i.e. nearly perpendicular to the court surface. It should be parallel to the net and impart a little bit of under-spin. Try to keep the head of the racket above the wrist, so

From the position of readiness, a small shoulder rotation takes the racket to the side of the body. With very little swing, the ball is struck firmly in front of the body by stepping forward to meet the ball. The follow through is kept short to enable a quick recovery. As shown by the circle in the drawing, the wrist is firm on impact.

get well down to low shots, by bending the knees.

There is often no time for footwork, but if there is the left foot comes down after ball contact, as the whole body-weight is transferred into the stroke. This compensates for the short take-back.

The follow-through is very short. It goes forwards. The player quickly then adopts the readiness position, to be well prepared for any subsequent shot.

If one is receiving a high ball, there is usually the opportunity for a more aggressive shot.

The lower the ball comes over the net, the lower the shot is executed, and the more defensive and controlled the shot has to be.

When lining up for the volley, the racket should be taken back in line with the ball as it is coming to you. This is important in maintaining a good centre of gravity for balance and it also ensures that you are able to watch the ball well.

One of the hardest volleys to make is the low volley. It is often the first volley and is made after the serve as the server is coming in to the net or perhaps sometimes when a volley is played from an approach shot.

As with all shots in tennis, one of the most important things in the volley is for the player to be on balance at the time of impact.

One of the greatest exponents of the volley in the present-day game is Stefan Edberg. He is very quick and hits the ball in front of him. Edberg's backhand volley is particularly good.

He hits the high ball very aggressively and controls the low ball to perfection.

The photographs on pages 112 and 113 show how well Stefan Edberg gets down to the ball, how his knees are well bent and, importantly, at the time of impact that he is on balance.

Once you have begun to master the return of the ball by volleying, do not remain content with a defensive or, at best, neutral shot. Whenever you have time, try to add impetus to the return, converting it into an attacking shot. If you are content just to get the volley back over the net, you often present your opponent with yet another chance to attack you. At the same time, one of the most common faults in the volley is that of players trying to do too much with the shot; they swing at the ball too much. In the earlier stages it is probably quite sufficient for you to place the racket head behind the ball, as long as the hitting point is in front.

Some Common Faults

In the volley common faults include:
  too much swinging at the ball
  hitting the ball too late – not far enough in front of the body
  dropping the racket head
  not bending the knees may be a contributory factor to dropping the racket head

13 The smash and the lob

The smash

For the smash the racket is held in a Continental, or semi-Continental, grip. The stroke can be thought of as being like a serve, but executed on the move. There is a similar 'throwing' action with the racket head, but there are also some very important differences. The pendulum movement of the serve action – the dropping of the racket head – is abbreviated because of lack of time, so that the racket tends to be brought upwards and backwards across the right-hand side of the body. The upper part of the body tends to be turned less sharply than for the service.

When playing a smash, keep the left arm outstretched and pointing upwards towards the flight of the approaching ball, following its path through the air. This gives an indication as to where you should position yourself in order to hit the ball. It provides visual assistance and at the same time it helps in lowering the right side of the body.

The looping action of this shot is less pronounced, because of shortage of time. The follow-through is also abbreviated just a little, with the racket finishing in front of the left-hand side of the body. It is important, as the ball comes to the player, that he moves his feet, getting his body to the side of the ball so that the hitting point is, as with the serve, just in front of the body and slightly to the right-hand side.

Usually, one has to move vigorously for the smash: it is not a static shot! That is the big difference between the smash and the serve. More often than not the player has to move in a backwards direction, in response to a lob. Sometimes a player is faced with a lob which would be higher than the fully extended reach of the racket, if the player remained with a foot on the ground. Thus the player has to leap upwards to ensure contact. It is not an easy shot because, whilst leaping, the body has to be under control. It is all a matter of co-ordination.

Good footwork is essential to get into the correct position for an overhead smash. Use small skipping steps so that, although moving in a backwards direction, the centre of gravity is kept forward. One of the problems for some players is that as they move backwards their whole body-weight moves backwards too quickly and they topple over. Good balance will also assist a quick recovery to be ready should there be a returned shot to deal with.

Ideally, the smash is a shot that one should try to 'put away' on the first attempt. When making this shot a player is often very close to concluding a point in his favour, and it is a great shame to throw away such opportunities. It is also often psychologically damaging. Care should be taken to avoid hurrying the shot and to concentrate on watching the ball. There is no point in aiming for the spectacular. The smash should be just fast and hard enough, penetratingly deep enough and sufficiently well positioned as to leave no possibility of a return

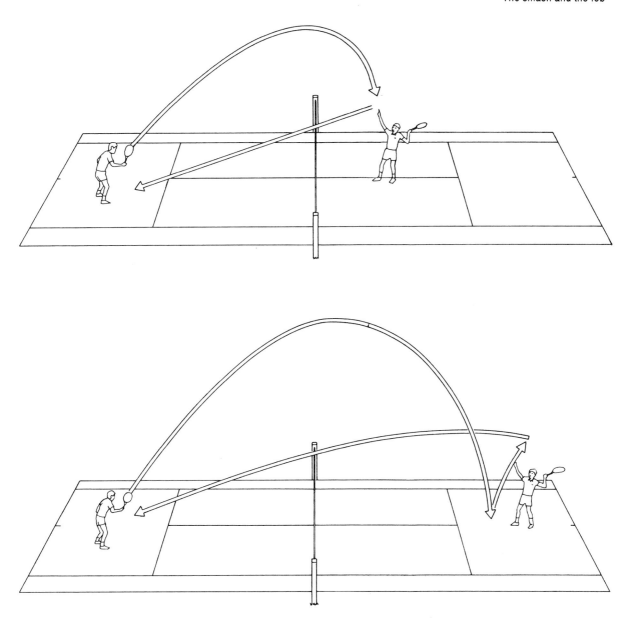

The smash: The higher the lob, the more vertical the drop of the ball and the more likely the player is to smash the ball after the bounce.

shot being made, without taking undue risks or expending unnecessary energy.

The backhand smash is one of the most difficult strokes in the whole game of tennis. It is a shot which few players perform well. It is usually executed whilst jumping because a high backhand volley would normally be played instead, if the feet were still on the ground. It requires a lot of strength in the wrist and lower arm. This stroke requires more body co-ordination than any other shot.

The sequence of this shot is that the racket is grasped in the Continental grip, or semi-Continental. The racket is inclined to be drawn back over the left shoulder. The upper body turns with the back towards one's opponent. It may help to visualize this by saying that if the player were wearing a numbered soccer shirt, then his opponent should be able to read the number. The arm is raised and the elbow high, pointing upwards. As the racket comes down over the shoulder, the left hand is used to support the neck of the racket as the shoulder turns. The player jumps off the ground and immediately stretches vigorously upwards, hitting the ball at the greatest possible height, with a flick of the wrist, so that the speed of the racket head is generated. The hitting point is slightly in front of the body and at the highest position possible. It is a difficult shot which requires a lot of body-turn and getting the body-weight into the ball with a powerful wrist-snap. It is this wrist action which really generates pace.

The drop-smash

Another permutation of the smash is the drop-smash. If your opponent's lob is very lofted, so that it seems likely that the ball would bounce

Anders Järryd, intently following the trajectory of the ball, adjusts his feet and turns sideways. He uses his left hand to enable him to get to the side and under the flight of the ball and, with a short swing, throws his racket at the ball in a fashion similar to the serve.

unusually high if it were allowed to do so instead of being smashed as it falls, then it may be better to let it fall and smash after it bounces. In this instance it is necessary to try to get into the same position as one would adopt for a serve. The only difference is that if the bounce is not as high as the ball-toss would be for the serve, then the player has to make height adjustments by bending his knees, so that the hitting point is still at the outstretched position of the arm. Thus the player is still using full height in terms of the stretch of the arm, but the hitting point has been adjusted by bending the knees. Otherwise, this drop-smash, or bounce-smash, is exactly the same as for the serve with the feet being used to get into that preparation position.

In making this split-second decision to elect for a drop-smash instead of the normal smash, you have to balance the probable greater safety in making the drop-smash and the greater amount of time to gather oneself and select the target area against the loss of attacking time and the chance for your opponent to scurry back into position while the ball bounces. There are also other considerations to be taken into account in this fraction of a second. These may include probable greater speed and easier attainment of depth from the volleyed smash, wind conditions and self-confidence in dealing with an extra high lob.

119

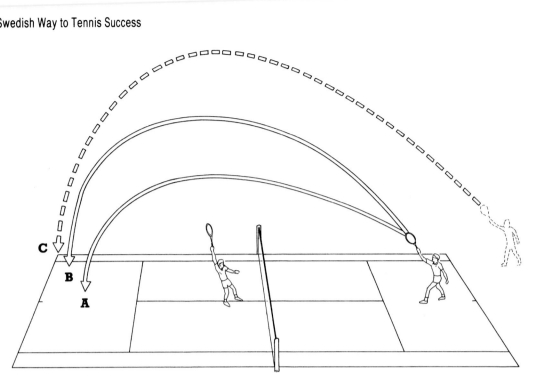

The three types of lob:

A The attacking flat lob: the flight of the ball just out of reach of the net player

B The attacking top spin lob: the flight of the ball with higher elevation dropping more abruptly

C The defensive lob: hit high and deep to allow time to recover.

The lob

It is appropriate to discuss the lob together with the smash, because although they may be very different in themselves, they are very often related, with the one being followed by your opponent using the other. A lob may bring forth a smash in reply, or a smash may result in a lob return.

The basic lob is a flat-hit shot. It is very much a variation of the ground-stroke, except that the elevation of the hit is higher. To do this, the player is using basically the same ground-stroke but opening the racket face a little bit to achieve the increased elevation of the shot. Thus the basic lob is similar to the ground-stroke except that the flight of the ball over the net is quite different. The ball must be as high as possible yet still land just within the court, the closer to the baseline the better.

The lob has become a very vital shot in the modern game. There are two variations of the basic flat lob: the offensive, or attacking, lob and the defensive lob.

In the offensive lob the ball must be struck much earlier than for a defensive lob and it must travel much more quickly over the head of your opponent. The elevation of the attacking lob, if it is made with a flat stroke, tends to be much lower. The ideal height to aim for is just above the maximum reach of the potential smasher as he takes position in the front area of his court.

The offensive lob which is now much used is hit with a great deal of top spin, and so is called the top-spin lob. Mats Wilander executes this shot extremely well, particularly on the backhand. His stroke pattern is such that it is very, very difficult to tell whether he is going to play a passing shot or hoist an aggressive top-spin lob. Jonas Svensson is another Swede who lobs well, particularly on the backhand.

The defensive lob is used much more to get oneself out of trouble. If your opponent is attacking the net position very quickly and you find yourself very deep or wide of the tram lines, the only way to get back into the middle of the baseline area, to stand any chance of playing the next shot, is to hoist a very high lob indeed. Thus the time which passes whilst the ball is in the air gives you time to get back into position. This shot has to be played high and it also has to land very deep in your opponent's court, close inside the baseline.

This shot is very similar to the flat lob, the difference being in the elevation. It helps to add a little bottom spin, or back spin, to such a defensive lob. This slice adds an extra measure of control over the lob.

Wind conditions need to be taken into account when making lob shots, especially very high ones. It is easier to lob into the wind than with a following wind. It is less advisable to choose to use the lob as an attacking stroke in unreliable, windy conditions.

14 Refined shots

The half-volley

The half-volley is played by the more advanced player. However, it is not a stroke which one naturally wants to play. A half-volley is usually forced upon you. It is also a difficult shot to execute.

Normally the half-volley is played as you are coming in towards the net, anticipating getting far enough in to play a volley, but your opponent plays the ball so well that it dips in front of you and you have to take the ball just off the bounce. That is the definition of a half-volley, a ball taken just after the bounce. It is not a fully-fledged ground-stroke, since it has an abbreviated swing. In fact half-volley is rather a misnomer because the shot is longer than a half-volley in terms of the stroke.

The half-volley is most often made in mid-court, or no man's land, where you are not far enough back to play a ground-shot nor far enough forward to produce a volley.

It is essential for this shot to bend the knees to get down to the ball. Take a short back-swing, hold the wrist firm and shorten the follow-through. The Continental grip is used most often as this shot follows directly after a serve. The forehand and backhand use basically the same technique, holding the racket firmly and hitting the ball out in front. It is seldom played aggressively as it is a control shot. In fact, the player tends almost to cradle the ball. It is important to be moving forwards, following-through and continuing to move towards the net. The whole body-weight and racket-head movement must be forwards.

This shot is not always played in the transition stage, moving from mid-court forwards. Sometimes it is executed near the baseline, when an opponent has actually played a shot harder, faster and deeper than anticipated. Then one is forced into playing a ball very quickly on the rise of the bounce. Some modern players have been able to play this shot with a slightly longer swing, from the back of the court with a little bit of top spin. This is a difficult shot to play. To do this, the face of the racket has to be a little more closed.

The half-volley is perhaps most useful during the very fast exchanges which take place near the net in doubles play, with all four players at net. There is then a considerable likelihood of a fast reply coming down at one's feet and leaving no time for any other shot. The half-volley return does carry with it a compensation, if successfully executed, in that it is winging its way back again into your opponent's court just that split second earlier from such a limited bounce.

The drop-shot

The drop-shot is played so that the ball just passes over the net and bounces as short as possible on the other side of the court, as close to the net as possible. It is played when one's opponent is out of court or out of position and it is something of a surprise shot. Generally, it is played with underspin, so that when it lands on the other side of the net it bites into the court and bounces low.

The mechanics of the drop-shot are somewhat the same as playing a sliced backhand, coming from high to low. The ball is hit firmly, but the racket face just glances the edge of the ball, almost tangentially. It is a touch shot and requires a great deal of racket-head control. This shot can be played from all parts of the court, but the further you are away from the net the more difficult the shot is to execute and the more you have to consider where your opponent is positioned at the opposite end of the court. There is no point in playing a drop-shot when your opponent is moving forwards, because if he reaches your drop-shot then you are totally vulnerable to his reply.

The important thing about the drop-shot is when to use it! Generally speaking, it is played so that your opponent is wrong-footed – he is moving in the opposite direction. The ball is played in the opposite direction to that in which he has initially commenced his movement. The most important feature of the drop-shot is to disguise it, so that your opponent fails to detect quickly enough just which shot you are going to play.

If you are on the receiving end of such a drop-shot, it is essential, prior to impact, to be on balance. Get to the ball as quickly as possible, then slow down and gain body control before the final execution of the shot. So often a player makes a valiant effort to reach the ball and succeeds in doing so, only to miss the reply.

In world-class tennis the drop-shot is now used more by women than men. Men players are physically so fast on the court that they can normally pick up a high-percentage of drop-shots.

The drop-volley

The drop-volley is dropped as short as possible on the other side of the net, from the volleying position. The tactics are the same for a drop-volley as in the drop-shot. The racket head cushions the ball as it comes off the racket. The mechanics of the shot are very similar to the normal volley, but sometimes the action of the drop-volley is described as 'turning the key'. Just like turning a key in a lock, the racket face is turned around the ball, taking the speed off the ball and imparting bottom spin to it, to give control and reduce its speed.

The lob-volley

The lob-volley is a specialist shot and occurs when both players are in the net position, exchanging volleys, and the decision is made that the best way in which to win the point is by placing the ball high over the head of the opposite net player. It is not an easy shot to execute. In fact it is a dangerous shot. If this shot is not played well, you become a clear target for your opponent. It is the opening of the racket face which creates the desired elevation. Once again, this is very much a 'touch' shot. It requires a great deal of 'feel'. The racket head comes round and underneath the ball, as the shot is played.

The knees need to be bent, the racket head held with the wrist firm and all of the basic coaching points connected with the volley apply, except that the racket head caresses the ball, taking the speed off it. The face of the racket is slightly opened to give the elevation that is required for the ball to fly over your opponent's head.

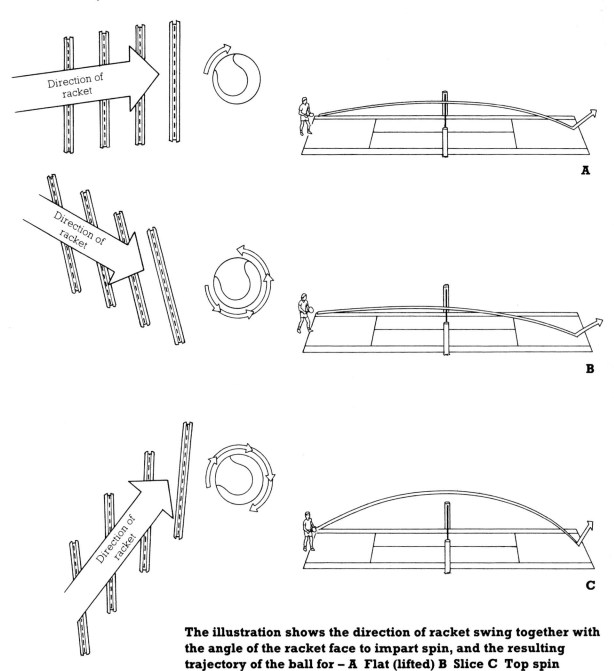

The illustration shows the direction of racket swing together with the angle of the racket face to impart spin, and the resulting trajectory of the ball for – A Flat (lifted) B Slice C Top spin

Spin

Imparting spin to the ball is in itself a refinement: the player can hit the ball high over the net, yet it still stays in play. For Björn Borg, the net ceased to be an obstacle. It was no longer something which was at all intrusive in the game. Top spin also allowed him to land the ball shorter in the court, as it would still be carried forward by the spin, which gives an added margin of safety. Top spin can also be used to dip the ball at the feet of an opponent near the net, forcing him to play a much more awkward volley. It also increases the angle for the passing shot giving yet another advantage. When used in combination with a lob, it makes the space above one's opponent more vulnerable.

Of course, accuracy of judgement is vital with top spin. A too low lob invites most aggressive retaliation and a too short ground-stroke allows an aggressive approach shot, particularly as its bounce is high.

Top spin also requires a lot more physical strength. Players who use this stroke rely less on timing and more on manipulating their own bodies, utilizing their wrists and their body strength.

Back spin is the opposite of top spin, and is imparted by striking downwards, from high to low. The advantage of back spin, or slice, particularly on a court which is low-bouncing, as on grass, is that the ball will stay down. This has a tactical advantage against a player who prefers a high-bouncing ball. He will find the slice difficult to handle.

It is also possible to impart side spin by drawing the racket face across the ball from one side to the other. This is far more likely to be from right to left on the forehand and, conversely, from left to right on the backhand. It is combined with a leaning of the body in the same direction as the racket face is drawn across the ball. This has the effect of accentuating the angle in which the ball is directed out to the side of the court.

15 Fundamental tactics

Tactics depend upon your own technical abilities and style of play. Obviously you cannot implement something that you are incapable of performing.

Tactics also depend upon your opponent's skills.

You need to assess your own abilities and those of your opponent. Ideally, you should consider both these things before you go into a match. You should try to identify the basic strategy that you are going to use, although obviously that strategy must be adaptable. Generally speaking, it is best to play your 'own' game first of all.

Probably the most important basic tactic is where you stand: from what position you play your strokes and to where you move your body in order to cover the court efficiently. Good positioning is very important. For example, when serving in singles stand as close to the centre of the baseline as possible so that you are equally well placed to deal with a returned shot on forehand or backhand sides.

Good positioning means placing yourself so that you are in the best situation in which to deal with your next stroke.

When rallying, you should be just behind the centre of the baseline. Coming too far forward will make you vulnerable to a deep shot from your opponent.

When serving and playing ground-strokes, it is important to keep the ball 'deep': to the baseline, in the case of ground-strokes and towards the service line, in the case of the serve. If you hit the ball short, you will give your opponent the chance to move forwards and play an aggressive shot or come into the net.

At all levels of play the outcome of a match is dictated by the errors made and not by the winning shots. Boris Becker has emphasized that success is gained not by the player who just manages to pull off some spectacular shot but by the player who keeps within the confines of what he is reasonably sure of achieving. It is therefore better not to keep your shots at a riskily low trajectory over the net and perilously close to the limiting lines. You can afford to allow to let the ball clear the net by as great a margin as a couple of metres (six feet) and this is made easier by the use of top spin to curve the ball down in the last stages of its flight.

A basic and obvious element of tactics is to put the ball where your opponent is not! In other words, to force your opponent to have to move. This will hurry his shot, giving him less time in which to get into position and play the shot which he wishes to play. It also contributes to the ultimate aim of tiring him.

As soon as you start hitting-up with an opponent in preparation for a match, you should try to assess his strengths and weaknesses. When you have discovered a weakness, you must then try to exploit it in your overall tactical plan. If you are a regular competitor, try to gain this information before the competition, rather than wait until the match

1.

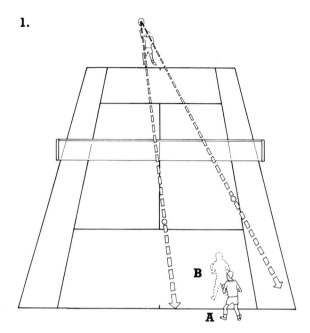

2.

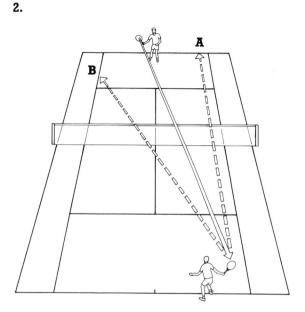

Court position 1 *Singles* – the receiver positions himself mid-way between the two extreme possibilities on the serve, down the middle or wide. Generally this is behind the baseline at A for the first serve, and inside the baseline for the second, weaker serve at B.

to discover those aspects of your opponent's game to be exploited. At the same time, however, one has to be cautious about playing to a weakness, because if you play to it too often or too regularly then that weakness perhaps grows stronger. Your opponent also becomes more ready for it and expects it. The added danger in over-concentration on a weakness is that you may yourself make more errors than necessary by altering course from your own more natural choice of shot.

Wrong-footing your opponent is a tactic that is particularly effective, especially on a slip-

2 Rally situation – the player again moves to a position equidistant to cover the two potential extreme shots, as indicated, either A down the line or B cross court.

pery court, such as shale or grass. This is a tactic that we all like to execute. When you see your opponent moving quickly in anticipation of a certain shot, push the ball in the opposite direction to the point from which he has just come. This catches him off-balance and often the best that he can achieve is an imperfect, uncontrolled shot. Although it may seem contradictory, the players who are most vulnerable to wrong-footing are often the quickest movers: they execute one shot and move on hastily to the next, anticipated shot, whereas the slower mover is in position for a longer time after hitting the ball, and is less easy to exploit.

The return of service should either be placed

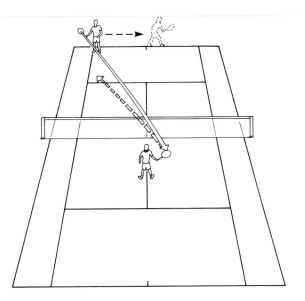

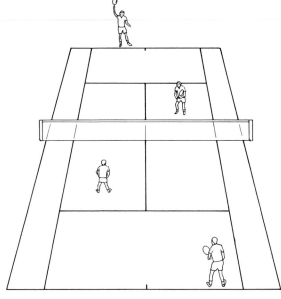

(Above) *Wrong footing* – a useful tactic, especially on a slippery court: seeing the opponent moving to the middle, return the ball behind them.

(Above) *Court position, doubles* – the basic court positions.

(Bottom Left and Right) *Approach shots down the line and cross-court* – note the placement of the approach shot. Clearly the

cross-court shot, opening up the court, increases the area not covered by the player.

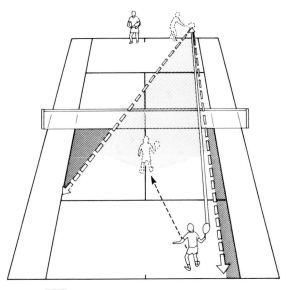

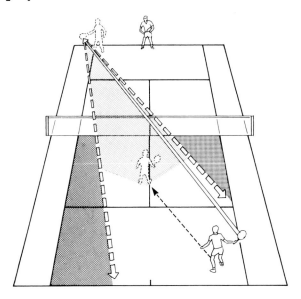

☐ Area of court covered by player

▨ Area of court not covered by player

deep into the court, if your opponent stays at the baseline, or low at his feet if he comes in and attacks the net position. The latter situation forces him to make a low volley and so this causes his shot to be lifted upwards and is therefore easier for you to attack.

Generally speaking more shots are played across the court than down the line. It is also easier to play a ball back along the path of its flight. But if you have the choice, play across court because you have the greatest distance to play with and the net is lower in the middle.

If you are faced with an opponent who likes to play to a fairly regular rhythm, try to prevent him from settling into the groove of his choice. You can achieve this by using variety of pace, of spin and of placement.

If you are leading in a game by 40–0 or 40–15, then you can take a chance; you can play slightly risky tennis. On the other hand, if the score stands at 30–30, the next point is obviously a very key one and you need to keep the outcome of it under your control as much as possible. You do not want to play shots which you know have a high risk. In these circumstances, you should play shots that you feel well able to control, at the same time making sure that your opponent cannot take the initiative. For example, if you are serving at 40–0 or 40–15 in your favour, then you can afford to attempt an ace. But at 15–30, against you, you would probably be better advised to put in a well-placed three-quarter paced first serve. Similarly, at 15–40, you would not wish to serve a ball wide to your opponent's forehand because by doing so, you are not only creating the angle for yourself but also one from which your opponent can reply with either a cross-court shot or an attacking shot down the line.

The illustration shows the way in which you can open up the court. If you volley or serve cross-court, you open up the angle quite considerably, thereby creating opportunities for your opponent.

If you are approaching the net, do so by following the line of the ball. By doing this, when you get to the net, you are in a better position to cover the responses from your opponent.

If a right-handed player places a forehand shot to his opponent's backhand corner, he should come to a net position just to the right of the centre of the court. This enables him to cover a potential passing shot down the line or a cross-court passing shot, with equal ease.

Keep the rally going in your favour and do not take too many risks. If there is an element of doubt, always play your most reliable shot.

To counter an opponent who is continually storming forward to try to dominate from the net position you have five options:

1 You can go for a passing shot down the line.

2 You can try a passing shot across the court.

3 You can play a lob.

4 You can play a shot that falls just over the net to bring your opponent closer to the net and probably force a defensive volley.

5 You can blast the ball directly at your opponent as he rushes in, so that he is faced with a ball which is aiming straight for him.

Your choice of shot must be governed by your assessment of your own ability to execute it successfully most of the time.

If from his attacking position at net your opponent forces you back, choose a lob as your most propitious shot. This may be a top-spin attacking lob, which after passing over the head of your opponent allows you to advance to a position at the net or a very high, defensive, sliced lob.

Doubles tactics

Doubles play is good fun and provides all-round training, even for the singles 'specialist'.

Doubles tactics are of course different, as there are two players to be considered on each side of the net. There is consequently less court area for each individual to have to cover. There is a very great advantage in getting up to the net, where most of the winning points are played. You should be far enough away from the net so as not to feel 'crowded' in that position, yet close enough to reach forward easily to it with a couple of close steps.

An illustration on page 128 shows you where players should stand in doubles.

The server is in a slightly different position from that adopted in singles, probably mid-way between the centre-mark on the baseline and the inner tramline. This allows the server to cover the cross-court return, which is the most likely shot. The server's partner usually stands mid-way between the inner tramline and the centre service line, approximately two metres (six feet) from the net, in such a position that he feels well able to cover his half of the court. That must include a potential shot down the tramlines or one down the middle, somewhat on his side. He must also be prepared to deal with a lob which might be put up by the receiver.

The receiver usually stands a little further back for the first service than the second. He moves forward in anticipation of the second serve and is most probably then standing just inside the baseline, with his outside foot quite close to the inner tramline. The partner of the receiver stands just inside the service box about mid-way between the inner tramline and the centre service line. He moves forwards if his partner returns the ball well.

The receiving pair have the choice as to which side of their court they stand to receive service and they retain that side throughout the set. With two right-handers (or two left-handers) the more solid, consistent player usually takes the deuce court (the right-hand side) and the other the advantage court (the left-hand side). Another consideration is that, as intercepting is so important, the best combined strength of volley needs to be in the middle.

Pairs which have a left-hander and a right-hander tend to play with the left-hander in the advantage court. Examples are Laver/Rosewall, Laver/Stolle, Roche/Newcombe and McEnroe/Fleming. The left-hander's forehand return, a more offensive shot, usually has greater effect and threat from the advantage court on key points.

The ability to make intercepting volleys is also of significance. Since it is easier to intercept with the backhand volley, having the left-hander in the advantage court makes sense.

There are exceptions: for example, one of the very best doubles pairs in the late 1980s, Pugh and Leach, who are right- and left-handed, have the left-handed Leach in the deuce court.

A weakness with the left-hander in the advantage court is that both backhands are in the middle and are vulnerable to the lob down the centre of the court. This problem is solved for Leach and Pugh: as Pugh plays both backhand and forehand with two hands, Leach is able to cover more of the middle in compensation. If these two players adopted the reverse sides, the middle would become much weaker.

In doubles, the first objective for the server is to advance to the net. The server in doubles usually does not serve as hard and fast as in singles. The slightly slower pace gives extra time in which to advance further towards the

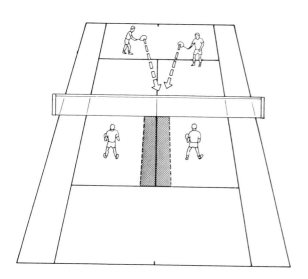

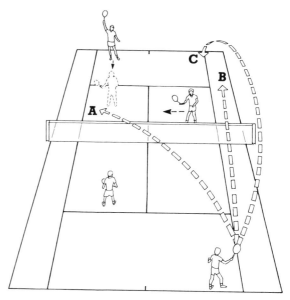

(Above) *Area of indecision* – the focus of most shots in doubles, showing the area of indecision.

(Below) *Australian formation* – both server and partner start the point from the same half of the court. The server moving, as indicated, to force the return down the line. This is called the 'Australian Formation'.

(Above) *Service return, doubles* – the possibilities on return of serve in doubles are A cross court at the feet of the incoming server B down the line past the player at the net C a lob over the player at the net.

(Below) *Planned interception* – both server and partner plan to change sides after the serve, as indicated, in an endeavour to cut off the return.

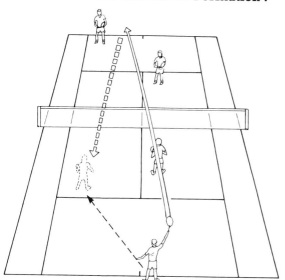

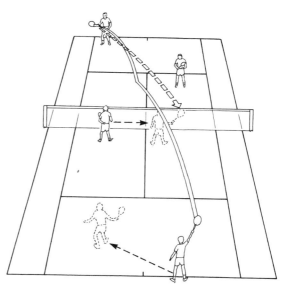

net, behind the serve. The most vulnerable area in doubles is down the middle, in the 'zone of indecision'. A high percentage of shots will be placed into this central area. This includes the serve as well, as this cuts out the angles.

The objective of the receiving pair, on the other hand, is to force their opponents back and away from the net. Normally, the receiver will try to return the ball much lower over the net than is the case with a return of service in singles, dipping the ball at the feet of the incoming volleyer. Hopefully, this will result in an enforced upwards volley giving the receivers a chance to take over the initiative with their own volley or smash.

Doubles is essentially a game of team-work,

the strengths of each partner complementing the other. In the Järryd/Edberg pairing, for example, Anders contributes his safe, low returns and fast reactions at net, whilst Stefan's reliable service often enables Anders to cut off shots at the net. Doubles pairs need to move together in unison on the court, so that they are able to cover the court in the most efficient manner. Doubles partners should imagine they are joined by a string attached to each of them so that they move at the same distance apart, whether forwards, backwards or sideways; they will then cover the court in the optimum way.

It also helps when partners complement each other temperamentally. It is generally recognized, for example, that Stefan Edberg has a calming effect on Anders Järryd, who somewhat uncharacteristically for a Swede has a shorter fuse.

A basic rule in doubles is that you cover your own lobs. So that if a ball goes over your head it is your responsibility to try to get back and deal with it, unless your partner calls for it, because he feels in a better position to do so. In the event of him doing so and thus switching sides, you should have a pre-arranged agreement that you will then automatically also switch to cover his exposed flank.

Communication between partners is very important: you must work together as a team.

Certain circumstances occur in doubles which require a tactical response. If your opponents are serving extremely well and you are having difficulty in playing an effective

Anders Järryd confidently controlling the net.

132

return to the feet of your opponents, you can try a lob. Or, your partner can stand back too, in what is called the defensive position, so that the return does not have to be so accurate. You could also try driving the ball down the line of the server's partner, particularly if he has been doing a lot of interception at net. This may force him to move out slightly to guard that wing of attack and so take some of the pressure off your other returns. The odd drive down the line will remind him of his need not to disregard that side of his responsibility at net. Even if your attempt is unsuccessful, it may well have the same reminding effect.

If, when you are serving, your opponents are returning very well, particularly cross-court, then you can change to the Australian formation. In this formation, the partner of the server stands on the same side of the centre line as the server himself. This more or less forces the returner to play his shot down the line – in other words, it breaks their rhythm.

Some doubles pairs use a planned interception tactic. The Americans Robert Seguso and Ken Flach, for example, change sides as soon as the serve has been hit.

These tactics are all designed with the intention of preventing your opponents getting into a successful groove and rhythm.

To be a good doubles player you must have the ability to serve and to return service accurately, and to get to the net quickly. You must also have quick reflexes so that you can take the opportunity to get the ball away at the net.

Anders Järryd has all these attributes. He also has the ability to 'read' the game very, very quickly and to react accordingly; this is a priceless gift since doubles is a very fast game.

PART 3

The Future of Tennis in Sweden
by Dennis Gould

16 Organizational structure of the Swedish Tennis Association

During the last two or three years the Swedish Tennis Association has been busily engaged in plans for a renovation of the Association upon the coming of the new decade. The project is called 'Tennis 90'.

Working groups have been dealing with the following aspects of the Association's activities:

Regulations and organization of Swedish tennis
Forms of competitions
Training, including Élite activities
Swedish women's tennis
Swedish tennis in breadth
Information

This preparatory work and the decisions subsequently made will affect the future of Swedish tennis.

Responsibility for dealing with the main aims for Swedish tennis are to be sub-divided between three blocks of committees:

Swedish Élite Tennis
Swedish Tennis Tournaments
Swedish Tennis in Breadth

In addition to these three operative blocks there is to be a Service Committee to support their work.

The specified tasks of the Governing Board and the committees are much the same as for similar associations, but set out below are the aims for the particular blocks of committees.

Swedish Élite tennis

During the nineties the targets are to retain Sweden's position as one of the top-ranking tennis nations in the world and at the same time to become one of the top four countries in women's tennis.

The committees forming this block are those for the Davis Cup, Federation Cup, Junior and Tretorn Tennis Academy.

Swedish tennis tournaments

The objectives of this group of committees are:

To provide all categories of players with an opportunity for competitive play
To co-ordinate the competitions
To introduce a fair ranking system
To create access to different forms of draw
To set up an information system for competition activities.

The committees in this block are Competitions, Handicap, Umpires and Referees, and All Swedish Series.

Swedish tennis in breadth

The STF aims:

To build 320 new indoor courts between 1989 and 1995
To have 250,000 members of Swedish Tennis by 1995
To have 500,000 tennis players by 1995
To develop so-called 'propaganda' tour-

naments for women, juniors and veterans.

This work falls to the committees of Club and District Development, Women's Tennis and Propaganda Tournaments.

Service Committee

This committee has the task of supporting the other committees and appropriate special areas of the work of the Board and Administrative Office.

There are also sub-committees for Training, Sponsorship, Law, Technical, Medical, Veteran and Medals. Some of these sub-committees may later be allocated to one of the blocks.

Swedish tennis will clearly be very much alive in the nineties!

17 Women's tennis

One aspect of Swedish tennis that has been conspicuous by its absence in this book is women's tennis. For the disappointing fact of the matter is that, as far as Swedish tennis success is concerned, Swedish women do not figure prominently.

Sweden's number one women's player, Catarina Lindqvist, had an unexpected success in reaching the semi-finals at Wimbledon in 1989. She is in forty-seventh position in the WITA ranking list. Maria Lindström, who is ranked number two, reached the quarter-finals of the Australian Open and Wimbledon in 1988. She is the only other Swedish woman in the top one hundred, in eightieth position. The next three in ranking order in Sweden are Maria Strandlund, Jonna Jonerup and Cecilia Dahlman, with Catrin Jexell and Maria Ekstand also in contention. After that, the most promising players are juniors.

For some time now, as the men started to make a name for themselves and then continued to do so, and whilst some of the spin-offs of that success were channelled into bringing women's tennis up with them, there has been disappointment over their failure. In Czechoslovakia and West Germany, two other countries where tennis has not had as long a tradition as in the United States and Australia, there has been a great upsurge in recent years. Ivan Lendl's successes have been matched by Martina Navratilova's and those of Boris Becker by Steffi Graf's. Catarina Lindqvist cannot be linked with the top Swedish men in this way.

Although there has been considerable concentration on developing women's tennis under Birger Falke, the well-known and respected Swedish tennis coach and former Davis Cup captain, so far his efforts and those of all who support him have not succeeded in producing a 'wonder' player.

There are many who have hailed Catarina's successes as a sign of the beginning of an advance. This may be an optimistic view, but a pessimistic angle has also been presented which draws attention to the fact that Catarina gained this success outside the normal pattern prescribed by those responsible for Swedish women's tennis.

For Catarina has adopted the hard approach which Lennart Bergelin has advocated. On her own initiative she elected to take part in the rough and tumble of life as a player in the US, and she has developed into a professional player with a dedication of the sort seen amongst the successful Swedish men players. Some critics have felt that the women have been too gently fostered. The situation was brought to a head when Sven Davidson came under some criticism for his 'tough' methods, which he believed to be necessary to get to the top. Catarina has been prepared to make an all-out

Catarina Lindqvist, Sweden's top woman player, semi-finalist in the Australian Open in 1987.

138

dedicated approach to the game. Judging by the drop-out statistics amongst the women as compared with the men, as presented by Tretorn Tennis Academy and the Report of research organized by the Swedish Pedagogic Institute, which set out to analyse the background and development of players, there is a less serious to be a professional among the women.

Sweden has been one of the foremost countries to champion the right of equality for women. Certainly and very understandably, however, there is a different sense of priorities as far as top tennis is concerned. Women seem to regard the game as a sport which they enjoy and play well, up until the point when other things appear to be more important and/or the recognition dawns that to strive for the very heights would demand too many sacrifices or that it is, quite simply, an impossible target. During a period around the middle of 1987 as many as 30 per cent of the 'best twenty' Swedish women withdrew from whole-hearted tennis.

There is perhaps some truth in the proposition that because Swedish girls are attracted to a wide range of sports there is a rather limited entry for tennis, whereby those with a certain talent find initial success all too easy. To gain local honours and then go on to be numbered among the leading Swedish women players has maybe not been such a demanding task. Progression to success internationally introduces new dimensions, including many of the less glamorous aspects of life on the tennis circuit. Not so many, up until now, have coped with that nor the relentless training this demands. Birger Folke has expressed his opinion that Swedish women must adapt their style to a more aggressive form to be able to succeed internationally.

Swedish women's tennis has yet to overcome the end of sponsorship by Volvo. But there are those who think that money is not necessarily the answer. It is felt that what is needed is a drive to attract many more girls to try tennis and then to choose it as their major sport. With a very much broader base at the point of entry, there should be a greater chance of more talent emerging to benefit from more concentrated coaching.

Working alongside Birger Folke is Nina Bohm, the former Swedish player who had the greatest potential before she was sadly forced to discontinue because of injury. She is far from giving up hopes for the future of Swedish women's tennis and the women's game features prominently in the Swedish Tennis Association's plans for the future.

⅄ Lessons for others?

When asked what were the factors contributing to the Swedish success, the coach of the Swedish Davis Cup team, Carl-Axel Hageskog, replied: 'A high standard of living which has made it possible for most people to be able to try out various sports, if they wish to. Good nourishment, positive home conditions and so on produce secure young individuals.'

The Swedish players are well-trained athletes who, within the limitations of injuries from time to time, are in tip-top physical condition. But this applies to almost all modern-day tennis-players who are striving to reach the upper ranking positions. The Swedes have no outstanding physical characteristic that is special to their nation. Just for the record, the heights of Borg, Wilander and Järryd are 180cm, 181cm, and 180cm respectively (i.e. all around 5ft 11in), Stefan Edberg is 188cm (about 6ft 2in). Thus, at 190cm (6ft 3in), young Niklas Kulti is an exceptionally tall Swedish player. They are all right-handed players.

The history of Swedish tennis shows that before Björn Borg there had been no remarkable tradition of world-class success in this sport. Nevertheless, Ove Bengtsson has included in his reasons for success 'a certain tradition within top Swedish tennis: i.e., a continuity within the national team from the twenties, through Kalle Schröder, Lennart Bergelin, Sven Davidson, Janne Lundqvist, Ulf Schmidt, Björn Borg, etc.'

How much of the success is due to coaching, either in the case of the individually successful players or up and down the country as a whole? Apart from the name of Björn Borg, coaching is one of the contributory factors most repeatedly mentioned by those involved in Swedish tennis as an explanation of Sweden's success.

What role does climate play, if any? When Australia and the US dominated the scene almost completely, about half a century ago, the British were often heard to make the inclemency of their weather an excuse. This was, of course, in the days when grass courts were much more in vogue. It is debatable to what extent that was a valid excuse in those long-gone days and moreover the Swedish climate is even more unfavourable.

But it is instructive to compare how Britain and Sweden have come to terms with the problems of climate. Britain seems largely to have ignored it, playing tennis on outdoors courts as weather conditions allow. And of course with the availability of grass courts and the chance of being able to play outdoors on En-Tout-Cas courts for many weeks of the year in Britain, covered courts were not such a necessity as in Sweden. But the Swedes, with typical thoroughness, have made the provision of indoor courts a top priority, making tennis a year-round sport. Certainly the mushrooming of covered court facilities in Sweden is a factor which has contributed to success.

Covered courts cost a considerable sum of money. What is the financial position of tennis in Sweden? Is it here that Sweden has the advantage? Do they have different priorities? Can investment of money produce results? Obviously, money alone is not the answer, but to what extent does it help? Has it helped Sweden? Jack Kramer, the well-known American expert on so many aspects of the game wrote in 1951 in his book *The Game* about American players getting very little official help. He made the point that, in France, in spite of the Tennis Federation having a three-million dollar budget to help with provision of a wide variety of support, development and incentives, this had not produced a single top player.

Swedish neutrality during World War Two led to Sweden entering the fifties with a higher standard of living than the rest of Europe. For a long time Sweden has been regarded as a shining example of the merits of a welfare state. They are generally known to have a very high rate of taxation, but they are also able to show the personal and communal benefits which these provide. It is also widely known that Sweden has had a virtually uninterrupted rule by a socialist government for half a century. But what is well-known is the fact that there has been less nationalization in Sweden than in Britain and that the capitalist wealth of the nation is very largely held in the enterprises of a handful of Swedish families. The combination of private sponsorship and community investment, with support by the state, has played an important role in the development of tennis in Sweden.

The three most successful Swedish players in recent years, Borg, Wilander and Edberg, all seem to have the ability to suppress their emotions on court. Is this a common element in Swedish temperaments or is it the result of conscious training? It is a national tendency to be introvert and coaches are aware of the advantages of self-control and concentration and try to cultivate and capitalize on these characteristics. It is a generally held theory, in Europe at least, that there is an association between temperament and latitude. There is a higher percentage of extroverts living in the warmer climes nearer to the Mediterranean. If there is any truth in their theory, then Sweden is certainly at the other end of the geographical and temperamental scale.

As a nation, the Swedes are also very thorough. Research, reports and statistics abound. It is not surprising therefore, that in 1985 the Swedish Tennis Association combined with the Pedagogics Institute in Stockholm to investigate the secret of tennis success in Sweden. A research group of sports pedagogues was established to examine and report on this phenomenon, which was called 'The Swedish Tennis Miracle of the Eighties'. Their aim was to try to explain how top Swedish players had achieved such great international success in recent years.

They set about this task by interviewing the five best Swedish male players and the five best Swedish female players. Their questions concentrated on background, experiences and development. Alongside this, as a control-group, they interviewed five men and five women of the same age-group who had been considered to be on a par with them, as far as achievement and potential were concerned, when they were all about twelve to fourteen years of age. But, in the case of the control group, these players had not achieved so well or had discontinued participation in serious competitive tennis. In addition the parents and the coaches of the successful players were interviewed.

These interviews indicate that even if the players in the control group were of the same level in their earliest teens they had attained it by dint of earlier maturity or through an earlier concentration on the sport. On the other hand, the players in the control group were less well-equipped psychologically to cope with what lay ahead of them. In this connection it became evident that shortcomings in the relationship or in regular contact with the same coach appeared to play an important part. Perhaps less obviously, even surprisingly at first, came the discovery that the environment of a large club tended to have a negative effect. In particular, the need to strive after qualifying standards at too early an age seemed to reveal itself as more off-putting than beneficial.

This latter attitude fits well into the general Swedish view of school-learning. With compulsory schooling not commencing before the age of seven years, there is a tendency to regard having to send British youngsters to school at the tender age of five as bordering on the cruel. Even at seven years, Swedish entrants have to pass a so-called 'maturity test' to determine that they are ready for schooling, and if they are so deemed, for the first term their hours of school attendance are far fewer than their British counterparts. Home coaching to prepare youngsters for reading, for example, is very much discouraged. So, if encouragement to get budding tennis-players onto the courts and into serious training at the earliest possible age appears now to be clearly against the evidence for success, this in no way conflicts with traditional Swedish educational tenets.

The findings of the Report, outlining the characteristics associated with the successful top players, can be summarized as follows:

1 They had good relationships with their parents, who demonstrated their support.
2 They grew up in smaller communities and had good opportunities to play more or less as and when they wanted.

3 They were good tennis-players in their early teens, but no better than many others of their own age.
4 Until the age of about fourteen, they were keenly active in a variety of sports.
5 Specialization in tennis began at about sixteen.
6 They received less coaching before puberty, but there was concentrated training later on.
7 They had a pronounced interest in competition.
8 They were mentally well-balanced.

The Report goes on to develop the idea of the psychological break-through when a player with whom one has probably trained or at least competed against in several national tournaments suddenly gains international success. It is possible for a 'barrier' to be removed and for a group of fellow players to move forward together to a new higher level. The success of one can inspire and boost the confidence of others: 'If he can do it, then I should be able to as well!'

There is no doubt that the success of Björn Borg created a whole new wave of interest in tennis among Swedes and a corresponding increase of input by the Swedish tennis authorities. However, there are many who claim that it was not just the sudden appearance of Borg that had such a carry-over value, but that the preparatory development of a structure which could support and encourage a long awaited upsurge of talent was already established. The system was prepared to capitalize on the subsequent benefits of the old adage that nothing succeeds like success. Those who make this claim are well supported by the evidence of the almost immediate follow-on of Wilander and then Edberg and the many others, after the passing of the Björn Born era.

19 The future of tennis in Sweden

Asked to comment about Swedish tennis in the next five years or so, Jonte Sjögren confidently replied: 'It will be very difficult to repeat but still I think Sweden will be a first-class Davis Cup nation. Players like Edberg and Wilander will stay "top-ten".'

The ability to maintain the almost incredible results of the past few years into the future is very much discussed, particularly in Sweden. Those who 'play the percentage game', so to speak, recognize that the odds of continued success at this level are stacked against the Swedes. Ove Bengtsson, for example, thinks the Swedes will lose more and more ground. There'll be a few 'stars' developing but not the depth at the top, as there is today. Sven Davidson has referred to the peak having been reached in 1988. Birger Folke feels that there will not be the same domination amongst the men as during the last five years. Perhaps Sweden will have two or three in the top twenty, but not more. He points to the small population of about eight million and says that there is no chance that Sweden will have so many super-talents as there have been. Jonas Svensson thinks that it will be difficult to keep up the same standard as before.

It should perhaps be stressed that those who express pessimism base it for the most part on Sweden's comparatively poor results in the Grand Prix events around the world during 1989.

But Sweden's position as a leading nation does not only depend on its own production of players. What is happening in tennis in the countries who are currently regarded as its strongest rivals will affect Sweden also.

Janne Lundqvist made the comment, after he had been commentating on Wimbledon in 1989 for Scandinavian TV, that he did not find one single new talent of whom he could say: 'Here we have a new star.' He felt that it was a bad omen for the future that players like Connors and McEnroe can still reach final rounds in major championships.

But those engaged in the attempt to stage a come-back in US tennis would certainly not agree with Janne, when the names of André Agassi and Michael Chang are now joined with John McEnroe, Brad Gilbert and Tim Mayotte, in the top ten. The USTA is planning to restore the past dominance which the US enjoyed in the tennis world. Millions of dollars are being invested in the striving to displace Sweden and other nations, such as Czechoslovakia and West Germany.

The USTA quite openly admit that they have been studying the successes and methods in other lands. It is not their intention to imitate any one country, but to pick the best from several and adapt those methods and ideas to suit their own conditions. It has to be fitted in to what already exists, such as the college system, which is more or less unique to the US. Perhaps the scientific investment from West Germany, the coach from Czechoslavkia, etc. etc. What is admired in Sweden, in particular, is the team spirit!

The well-known tennis ace, Stan Smith, leads the US national coaching team. Their intention is to nurture a couple of thousand players, approximately equally divided between the sexes, with an average of twenty in each of the many nation-wide training centres. Forty or more of the most promising will be selected for a youth team and will follow the kind of programme which has proved so successful in Sweden, with Team SIAB.

The Americans must take great heart from the performances of some of their young players. Yet younger and younger players are producing impressive results. Incidentally, however, of the five male international players who have won Grand Slam titles as teenagers, three have been Swedes. Apart from Borg, Wilander and Edberg there were Becker and Michael Chang, the youngest winner of them all. Towards the end of 1988 the USTA National Boys' 18 years singles title was won by Tommy Ho, at the age of only fifteen. He is the youngest-ever winner of the tournament which is approaching its seventy-fifth anniversary. But even more remarkable was the success of twelve-year-old Jennifer Capriati who won the USTA National Girls' 18 years title.

At the beginning of November 1989 the US took over the position of leading tennis nation from Sweden. In the top twenty of the ATP rankings for men, there appeared no less than nine Americans. McEnroe, Agassi, Chang and Gilbert held fourth, fifth, sixth and seventh positions respectively.

It is not to be expected that the Australians are likely to be happy with their slide into a considerably less important international position than they held for such a long time. They won the Davis Cup every year, except three, from 1950 to 1967, and each of those defeats was by the US. Pat Cash's Wimbledon win in 1987 may very well help to give inspiration to those making efforts to effect a come-back. It is interesting to note that one of the young Australian hopes, winner of the boys' singles in the 1988 Australian Open, was Johan Anderson, a Swedish immigrant.

But apart from the challenge from old giants of the game, such as the US, there are other countries in Europe struggling to emulate the kind of reputation which Sweden has achieved. Similar countries with a fairly lengthy but rather indifferent tradition produce stars now and again, but with no real depth of top-ranking talent. The Swedes have long been well aware of the challenge from Czechoslovakia, but they were given a sharp reminder in Båstad in the summer of 1989 when fourteen-year-olds from that country more or less dominated their age-group. Filip Kasak beat the highly regarded young Swedish hope, Thomas Johansson, in straight sets and at 6–0 in the second. In the girls' section the final consisted of two Czechs playing against each other. Another sign of Czech strength was evidenced in a new event introduced to celebrate the great Australian coach, Harry Hopman, and played for the first time in December 1988. National teams consisted of one male and one female representative. Catarina Lindqvist and Mikael Pernfors represented Sweden, but finished as runners-up to the Czechs, who were represented by Helena Sukova and Miloslav Mecir. Mecir thus emphasized the validity of the nickname which he has earned in tennis circles, after an impressively high percentage of wins against Swedish players in particular. About five seasons ago, in twenty-two matches against ten different top Swedish players over a period of around a year and a half, he only lost three of them. He is known as the 'Swede-basher': unfortunately the full significance of this play on words is lost in translation in Sweden, where he becomes the 'Swede-killer'.

Although more than a quarter of the Grand Prix victories on clay during 1988 were achieved by Swedish players, the Czechs also did increasingly well. Argentina was on a par with the US. In fact over the last two decades, Argentina comes second to Sweden in GP wins on this particular surface. The strength of the challenge which may be expected from Argentina is also reflected in the NEC junior world rankings. Although the Swede, Niklas Kulti, heads the boys' section, the only country with two players named in the top ten of September 1989 is Argentina. Their girls are stronger still in first and third positions. South American tennis is certainly thriving outside Argentina as well, with four other girls in the top twenty, representing Brazil (two), Chile and Venezuela. It is also noteworthy that it was an Argentinian, Alberto Mancini, who took the Monte Carlo title in 1989, where he beat Boris Becker. Monte Carlo has been a favourite place for Swedish players, both as a tax haven and for its most beautiful setting, but it has also seen seven Swedish triumphs by a variety of players since Borg first won in 1977. Last time, though, Mats Wilander succumbed to this promising twenty-year-old Argentinian. Undoubtedly, the well-known figure of Guillermo Vilas is a great support and inspiration for the Argentinian challenge for even higher world ranking. At one and the same time their hopes were raised and those of Great Britain denied when the South Americans were victorious in a match to decide which nation should go forward into the Élite Division of the Davis Cup Tournament in 1990.

However, in the long term, there is also great interest in the possible development of countries which do not have much past tradition to speak of, such as the Soviet Union, East Germany and even China.

Two additional recent factors could affect the competitive scene of tennis. One is the increased political liberalization with its opening up to interests in the Western World coupled with an easing of travel and interchange. The other is the re-introduction of tennis into the Olympic Games, after an absence of sixty-four years. However regrettable in some ways that it may be, the Olympic Games are used to reflect more than the prowess of the individual competitors, but are accompanied by national glory which can be derived from it. This fact may well lead nations new to tennis to concentrate their undoubted athletic talents and vast pools of population in this direction.

Participation in the Olympic women's events was very strong, with most top-ranking players being present. The reigning Wimbledon champion, Steffi Graf, won the Gold Medal. She ranked that as a more satisfying achievement than winning Wimbledon. But there was not such an involvement on the men's side. There were high Swedish hopes when Stefan Edberg reached the semi-final, there to meet his by now familiar rival in important matches, Miloslav Mecir. This time the Czech player was victorious and Stefan had to content himself with the Bronze Medal. Similarly, in the men's doubles, Edberg and Järryd did not reach the high standards that their Swedish supporters had come to expect of them and they, too, collected Bronze Medals. However, these events in the future will still attract strong entries from many of the world's leading tennis countries and will attract new ones.

As far as the USSR is concerned, their players are not unknown on the international circuit. It is, after all, now nearly thirty years since the USSR first participated in the Davis Cup competition. In 1973 Metreveli reached the Wimbledon final and the following year Olga Morozova did the same, in the women's tournament. Andrej Tjesnokov is currently ranked as number eighteen in men's tennis and Natalia Zvereva is at number fourteen, and there are two other Soviet women in the top forty.

With about forty times as many people to choose from as the Swedes, it is not impossible that Soviet players will be seen more and more, if that country sets its sights on success in tennis. But the current facilities available in the country make it seem very unlikely that their optimistically expressed target of a handful of Soviet players in the top rankings by the middle of the nineties will be realized.

East Germany has less tradition even than the USSR, but we have all seen what this country can do in branches of sport to which it puts all the state's powerful, concentrated effort. The recent startling political changes and increased contact with West Germany may result in surprising changes in tennis too; and sooner than otherwise expected.

China has two things greater than the Soviet Union: greater numbers of people and greater lack of facilities. It will probably be a long time before even the visits of Percy Rosberg and Björn Borg to that country produce results which constitute a serious threat to Swedish tennis.

During their recent visit to China, Percy and Björn expressed surprise at the standard achieved by the Chinese players, considering the very poor facilities available. Yet, in spite of a lack of courts and equipment, probably their greatest need is that of coaches. The Chinese are keen to send their players and few existing trainers to Sweden and Percy is planning a return to help coaches and junior players.

As yet, Japan has not turned its fanaticism towards tennis. But if tennis follows in the wake of golf in Japan, the present high standards and riches there, linked to dedication and organization, could produce surprises in this sport too. Already, in the NEC junior world rankings for girls, two Japanese names appear in the top twenty with the highest in eighth position.

But, for the time being at least, Sweden can be very satisfied with its comprehensively good results and rankings compared with other nations. In 1988 Wilander led in Grand Slam tournaments and Hardcourt Championships. Edberg was first in Grass and Indoors. On Clay, Kent Carlsson held the best Swedish position at fifth.

The 1989 picture shows less Swedish dominance. Lendl has taken over the two first places held by Wilander and Becker has replaced Edberg in the two leading positions that he held. On Clay, Carlsson has slipped to tenth but Edberg and Wilander have come in at sixth and seventh. But this latter encouragement to Swedes may be reduced for those who recall the comment made last year (when the Swedes did less well on Clay), that Clay Tournaments are beginning to become less prestigious amongst top players. The best Swedish results are to be found in Grand Slam events with Edberg second and Wilander equal third. Indoors, the best Swedish placing is Edberg at seventh. Wilander is second on Hardcourt with Edberg sixth, whilst on Grass, Edberg is third and Wilander fifth. Under normal circumstances these would be remarkable achievements for such a small nation, but after the glittering successes of the past they now pale slightly.

Looking ahead to the future, the shrewd observer and commentator on Swedish tennis Bengt Grive (a one-time table-tennis champion)

considers the ability to adapt to different surfaces is a pointer to real talent; he sees Peter Lundgren as a possible link-man between the era after waning current stars and the up-and-coming youngsters. It is Grive's opinion that Lundgren has a great deal of potential. The comparative rareness of this talent for adaptability is demonstrated by the fact that apart from Jimmy Connors, Mats Wilander is the only player to have taken singles titles in events at Grand Slam level on hard court, clay and grass. In the case of Lundgren's talents, indoor surfaces replace clay.

Whilst there is obvious concern for Sweden's tennis future, particularly since the senior men players did far less well in the early part of 1989 compared with the marvellous results of the previous year, there are those who are far from disappointed with the signs for the coming years which are reflected in the Junior European Championship results.

As far as younger players are concerned, the current hopes for future successes amongst the juniors are linked with the names of Niklas Kulti, number one in the 1970–1 age group; Johan Alvén, number one in the 1972–3 group; Tomas Enqvist number one 1974–5 and Thomas Johansson, who is in the same age-group but is a year younger. From 1976 there is Percy Rosberg's prodigy, Magnus Norman.

Thomas Johansson won the singles title and so became the best fourteen-year-old in Europe. This honour has also been held by Mats Wilander, Stefan Edberg, Kent Carlsson,

Kent Carlsson, one of the young Swedish players who has come to excel on clay courts.

and more recently Niklas Kulti. This is obviously an encouraging sign. In addition to young Thomas's first international gold medal there was a long list of silver and bronze medals winners, and the eighteen-year-olds won the European team championship. At the same time as expressing great satisfaction over gaining overall second place behind Czechoslovakia, in a points count for the championship, the Swedes also drew attention to the fact that after winning junior Wimbledon, Niklas Kulti was concentrating on senior events and did not play as a junior, and nor did the number one ranked sixteen-year-old, Johan Alvén. The best Swedish eighteen-year-old girls were also absent from this junior event.

Amongst those responsible for Swedish junior tennis there is no recognition of any need for anxiety. On the contrary, they consider Sweden to be well in the top ranks of international junior tennis.

In the transition from junior to senior is Niklas Kulti; the 190cm (6ft 3in) tall Swede. He has followed in Stefan Edberg's footsteps by being acclaimed Junior World Champion. He did not quite match Stefan's unequalled Grand Slam in boys' singles, as he was only victorious at Wimbledon and in Australia. He was hoping that a win at the US Open would offset, to some extent, only having reached the quarter-finals in France, but he disappointed himself by losing in the finals of the US Open. Nevertheless, he has every right to be acclaimed as 1989's most outstanding junior player.

That still left him with another ambition for the season: to finish up in the top one hundred ATP rankings. At the time when there were still two months of the year left, he still had about thirty places to climb and only a handful of younger players with better ranking. Meanwhile, Niklas is under the careful supervision of Martin Bohm. Martin is the captain of the Swedish junior Davis Cup team. In addition to Niklas there are nineteen-year-old Magnus Larsson (another tall, hard-hitting player) and eighteen-year-old Johan Alvén. Whilst recognizing the near impossibility of retaining the incredible recent Swedish tennis achievements, Martin is determined and optimistic about Sweden remaining amongst the leading tennis nations. He insists that any present-day stagnation is only temporary. He is waiting for a similar spin-off effect to that which accompanied the successes of Borg and Wilander, as Kulti and Co. climb higher. He also praises the immense encouragement that the up-and-coming young players receive from the established stars; in 1989 for example, no less than sixteen Swedes competed simultaneously at major tournaments in Australia and they were like one big, happy family.

But, if we leave future hopes and return to the present, there is little doubt that a great deal depends on Mats Wilander. He is young enough for it to be said that he is about half-way through his tennis career. Will he have the motivation and desire to continue in a sport where there are few more personal honours left to be achieved? During the rather barren year of 1989 there have been regular comments from Mats himself, and these have been reiterated by Jonte Sjögren, that Mats is feeling more motivated again and a come-back is imminent. Towards the end of 1989 it also became generally known that Mats's father had been very seriously ill and this had been preying on his mind.

As it became known that Sweden was to meet Germany in the Davis Cup final for the second successive year, it was recognized that Mats's input could well have far-reaching consequences as far as Sweden's tennis future is concerned. In this connection there was especial interest in his performance in the Stockholm Open, to which he came after a comparatively poor season and fresh from yet another disappointment, having been beaten in Paris by the up-and-coming Argentinian, Alberto Mancini in two straight sets, albeit 10–8 in the first set tie-break. This was after Mats had had a two months' break.

Perhaps hopes for Mats were raised when his club-mate, Jan Gunnarsson, from Växjö, caused a great sensation by beating Boris Becker. After such excitement and little sleep during the sixteen-hour interval before Jan had to play against Mats, it is probably not surprising that Mats proceeded to the next round quite comfortably. He then faced another compatriot, Magnus Gustafsson, who had also brought off a surprise victory over the greatly acclaimed Agassi, 6–3, 6–1. It almost seemed as though fellow Swedes were conspiring in an effort to smooth Mats's way towards the final and produce a much needed confidence booster for both Mats and the Davis Cup team. At the press conference, after beating Jan, Mats joked, 'It seems a long time since I won three consecutive matches.' On paper the odds were strongly in his favour to beat Magnus. Gunnarsson had only one previous Grand Prix title to his credit, whereas Mats had thirty-two.

But Mats's winning streak was to be short-lived. Magnus won the first set at 10–8 in the tie-break. The second set commenced with three successive breaks of service, after which Magnus held his service to lead 3–1. From then he held on until his final victory over Mats, with 6–4 in the second set. In 105 minutes Magnus Gustafsson had defeated the number one world ranking player of 1988 to enter the final of the Stockholm Open.

It has been said about Mats Wilander that he needs to be playing full-out and to be inspired. He has three great qualities which have combined to bring his success: consistency, a strong psyche and physical stamina.

His consistency was evidenced in his winning the five-hour-long match in the final of the US Open in 1988 against Ivan Lendl. His coach and mentor, Jonte Sjögren, commented afterwards that Mats only hit two bad shots during the whole match. Even allowing for a little prejudice, Mats undoubtedly played a most consistent match.

His strong psyche has been exemplified in the manner in which he won over Pat Cash, in the Australian Open final. During the extreme tensions of the decisive fifth set and in front of a largely Australian crowd of spectators, it was his mental strength which tipped the scales in his favour.

His stamina was shown at its best in the semi-final of the French Championship. In a test of endurance against the young American, Agassi, it was Mats who better stayed the course. His physical stamina prevailed.

Mats has also been described by John McEnroe as the player who 'reads' the game best.

A combination of these qualities in a player with Mats's experience must surely be hard to overcome. Perhaps the person who will most easily put an end to Mats's reign at the top of men's tennis is Mats himself.

Maybe the Swedish policy of concentrating on 'broad tennis' in the nineties and spreading the idea of 'tennis for fun' is rather timely! Perhaps it is a comforting thought for the British, who have had to be content with minimal international tennis honours for quite a few decades now. Our only consolation in recent years has been that we play tennis for the sheer joy of it!